## Praise for *Extraordinary Canadians*

"This collection of greats is astounding. It shows what Canadians do: we think of others and act selflessly, and with great and quiet courage. As I read through these pages, I felt that each person formed infinite branches of an eternal maple tree, flickers of the flame that burns bright upon Parliament Hill and within the hearts of all of us."

Jesse Thistle, #1 bestselling author of *From the Ashes*

"Three words describe the Canadians whose stories are told in this book: *courage*, *resilience*, and *imagination*. The courage to face the unthinkable and take on the impossible. The resilience to pick up when things go wrong and carry on. And the imagination to find new ways of living and giving. These heroes, sung and unsung, teach us what it is to be a Canadian. An entertaining and uplifting read."

Beverley McLachlin, former Chief Justice of Canada and bestselling author of *Truth Be Told*

"[A] remarkable collection of personal stories about Canadians, many of them unknown to the wider national community, who have helped make this country a better place for all."

*National Post*

"A feel-good, inspiring read."

*Toronto Star*

"*Extraordinary Canadians* is a book about extraordinary Canadians written by an extraordinary Canadian. Everything about it is extraordinary. Some would say that to brag about being extraordinary is un-Canadian. I say, it's time we celebrated ourselves. But what do I know? I wasn't extraordinary enough to be included in this book. Screw you, Peter."

Mark Critch, comedian and bestselling author of *Son of a Critch*

"[A] wide range of inspiring stories from the perspective of seventeen Canadians who aren't necessarily well-known but have made a difference in their own ways across the country."

*The Canadian Press*

"One of the book's many strengths is the way the authors let their subjects discuss their achievements within the full context of their lives, alongside failures, frustrations, and disappointments of all sorts. The achievements are diverse in nature but share a theme: they found their strength and calling in fighting conditions that initially seemed insurmountable. The range and diversity of the subjects is a tribute to their legwork—and the composition and diversity of this country. It is, in essence, a love letter to his country."

*Policy Magazine*

"A welcome exposure to an abundance of goodness afoot in Canada . . . Fresh and illuminating . . . The book especially deserves its own stamp of 'extraordinary.' "

*Winnipeg Free Press*

**Peter Mansbridge with Mark Bulgutch**

*Extraordinary Canadians*

**Peter Mansbridge**

*Peter Mansbridge One on One: Favourite Conversations and the Stories Behind Them*

*Off the Record*

**Mark Bulgutch**

*That's Why I'm a Journalist*

*That's Why I'm a Doctor*

*Inspiring Canadians*

# HOW CANADA WORKS

## The People Who Make
## Our Nation Thrive

—————————◆—————————

# PETER MANSBRIDGE
### AND MARK BULGUTCH

**PUBLISHED BY SIMON & SCHUSTER**
*New York   London   Toronto   Sydney   New Delhi*

SIMON &
SCHUSTER
**CANADA**

A Division of Simon & Schuster, LLC
166 King Street East, Suite 300
Toronto, Ontario M5A 1J3

Copyright © 2023 by Simon & Schuster Canada

This Simon & Schuster Canada edition November 2024

SIMON & SCHUSTER CANADA and colophon are registered trademarks of
Simon & Schuster, LLC

Simon & Schuster: Celebrating 100 Years of Publishing in 2024

For information about special discounts for bulk purchases, please contact Simon &
Schuster Special Sales at 1-800-268-3216 or CustomerService@simonandschuster.ca.

Manufactured in the United States of America

10  9  8  7  6  5  4  3  2  1

Library and Archives Canada Cataloguing in Publication

Title: How Canada works : the people who make our nation thrive / Peter Mansbridge &
Mark Bulgutch.
Names: Mansbridge, Peter, author. | Bulgutch, Mark, author.
Description: Simon & Schuster Canada edition. | Previously published in 2023.
Identifiers: Canadiana 20240344723 | ISBN 9781668017180 (softcover)
Subjects: LCSH: National characteristics, Canadian—Anecdotes. | LCSH: Helping
behavior—Canada—Anecdotes. | LCSH: Altruism—Canada—Anecdotes. | LCSH:
Employees—Canada—Biography. | LCSH: Canada—Biography. | LCGFT: Anecdotes. |
LCGFT: Biographies.
Classification: LCC FC641.A1 M36 2024 | DDC 971.07092/2—dc23

ISBN 978-1-6680-1718-0
ISBN 978-1-6680-1717-3 (hc)
ISBN 978-1-6680-1719-7 (ebook)

*For my parents: Brenda and Stanley*
*They, too, helped make Canada work*

# Contents

# Introduction

In the 1990s, I was driving from Toronto to my cabin in the Gatineau Hills on the Quebec side of the Ottawa River. It was early on a glorious late-spring morning, and the sun was shining. There was hardly anyone on old Highway 7 near Perth, Ontario, and I was singing along, badly I'm sure, with my radio. And I'll admit, I was pushing the speed limit.

At that time, I had been the anchor of *The National* and the chief correspondent for CBC News for almost a decade. It was a great job, working alongside dedicated colleagues determined to share with Canadians a clear-eyed and unbiased look at the news each day. I still had to pinch myself every morning to believe the job was actually mine. It had taken me across Canada, from coast to coast to coast, and around the world, and allowed me to meet some of the most famous people on the planet. I had been lucky enough to win several journalism awards. I was recognized almost every time I went out, which was a strange thing for an introvert to handle, but I was always grateful to the people who cared about the work we were doing and who wanted to talk about our country and the world.

As I was driving down Highway 7, my foot a little heavy on the pedal, I don't remember what I was thinking. I'm sure it must have been about work, as I was always thinking about work. I certainly wasn't thinking about the speedometer.

Suddenly, I saw flashing lights in the rearview mirror and heard the familiar sound of a siren. A police officer was signalling for me to pull over. There weren't any other cars on the road, so it was obviously me he was after. Not a good feeling.

I slowly pulled onto the gravel shoulder on the side of the road and, anticipating what would happen next, leaned over to the glove compartment and began to gather my essential documents: driver's license, registration, and insurance. I lowered my window as the officer walked up to the side of the car. He got straight to the point.

"License and registration, please."

I remember he was in sunglasses. Okay, maybe I made that up. They always wear sunglasses in the movies. But it's my story anyway.

He looked at me. And my papers. And my license.

He studied the license for a moment and then took off his sunglasses—dramatic pause—and said with an air of surprise, in fact, almost excitement, "Peter Mansbridge!"

I felt the tension release from my body. *God, I love this job.*

I smiled. He smiled back.

"We were in Sea Scouts together in 1962 in Ottawa!" he said.

Wait. What? I thought back. Yes, I had been in Scouts in Ottawa in 1962, and though I didn't remember him, I said: "Of course, yes, I remember."

We laughed and chatted about the names we recalled and the trips we took, stretching our minds back to those carefree teenage days. It was almost friendly. Until we ran out of things to say.

Then, there was a pause.

"So, Peter, what do you do now?" he asked. And then he gave me a ticket.

I tell that story often. In fact, I told it two years ago in my last book, *Off the Record*, a collection of anecdotes, some funny like that one. But I tell it here for a different reason. It makes me realize how connected so many of us are to our jobs, and how our jobs are a part of who we are, me included.

By the time I was seventeen years old, I had given up on high school and began a series of jobs. The first was as a counsellor and lifeguard at an all-boys summer camp, where I eventually became waterfront director. Then I joined the Royal Canadian Navy and went into the pilot training program with dreams of being a Top Gun of sorts, but Tom Cruise I wasn't. After leaving the Navy, I travelled from my last base in Portage La Prairie, Manitoba, to Ottawa, where I got a job as a gas station attendant at Roy Rump's ESSO station at the corner of Island Park Drive and Richmond Road. I learned the secrets of serving the public while ringing up the till. There was little profit on gas sales themselves, but there was 50 percent or more profit on everything else. So when you set the pump to fill slowly—there was no self-serve back then—you had lots of time to check the oil, sell window washer fluid, air filters, and if you were really good, maybe notice the tires were getting a bit bald on the edges. I was good. Roy used to brag to his pals about just how good I was. The hours were long, and days off were rare. I still remember how we'd all joke about what ESSO really meant: Every Second Saturday Off.

But my girlfriend was out west, so I headed back to the prairies. It wasn't long before I was not only out of work but also out of money. One day, while sitting in the bus depot in Winnipeg, I noticed a newspaper ad: TRAFFIC AGENT WANTED. And I thought, "Why not?"

The job interview led me to short stints as a baggage handler, ticket agent, and sometimes flight announcer for the regional airline, Transair, in Brandon, Manitoba; Prince Albert, Saskatchewan; and finally, Churchill, Manitoba.

By a fluke, it was a CBC radio executive hearing my voice announcing flights that got me my next job as a late-night radio host, which led to a series of jobs, first as a reporter in Winnipeg, then as *The National*'s correspondent in Regina, a parliamentary correspondent in Ottawa, the weekend anchor in Toronto, then the full-time anchor, and finally to chief correspondent of CBC News. Go figure. I don't think they had a human resources department checking qualifications in those days!

That title of chief correspondent is second only to one other title in my life: Dad (and now Grampy).

But I earned and lived that title as a core part of my being. And that's what I try to get to in this book. For so many of us, our jobs matter to who we are as individuals, as members of a community, as people who live and contribute to society, as Canadians. But the jobs we have make Canada work. That's right, they make Canada work. Let me explain.

When my family immigrated to Canada in the mid-1950s, I was just six years old. My parents spent a lot of time trying to convince my sister and me how great Canada was and how we would quickly come to love it. In making his case, my father used to point to a map and say, "Peter, look how big Canada is!" And seeing as we'd come to Canada from England and what was then Malaya, it sure looked a lot, lot bigger than where we'd left.

"But it's more than size. Canada is so different in its parts," he'd explain, "but it still works."

Geography, language, culture, regional differences on all kinds of issues. But it still works. He'd talk about not getting fooled by the loudest voice arguing that the country didn't work. He'd wax on about the great Canadian tradition of compromise, and perhaps most importantly, about how the majority of Canadians just go about their day, doing their thing, doing their job. *They* make Canada work, he'd say. My sister would take it all in. I, on the other hand, wasn't convinced. Show me, I'd think. If we Canadians are, as the old saying goes, a sum of our parts, and that sum was positive, then I wanted to see it.

Almost seventy years of crisscrossing the country have given me that opportunity. And I can confidently say now that my father was right.

When Mark and I started talking about a new book to write together, we looked back at our first joint production. *Extraordinary Canadians* in 2020 resonated with readers because it told Canadians about some very special people: people who made a difference, often when they faced a major obstacle in their lives and refused to back down. Through us, they spoke about how they handled challenges, and in doing so, their stories have inspired others and made a difference in many other lives.

In this book, we take it a step further. We try to understand extraordinary individuals in light of not only who they are but what they do. When we think of what makes this country *function*, it's the jobs—both big and small that help us run our lives each and every day—but what makes Canada *work* are the people doing those jobs.

Early in the Stephen Harper majority government of 2011, I had breakfast with one of the prime minister's top advisors, Kory Teneycke, who told me, "The problem with the legacy media is you are missing what real Canadians are talking about. You spend so much time drinking your own bathwater, you don't listen to what real people in different parts of the country are saying about their lives." I've never forgotten that friendly lecture and have tried to use it in practice, and I'll try again here.

And so, you won't find politicians, business leaders, celebrities, or—and I say this carefully—activists in this book. That's not to say none of those people are worthy, but it is to say that's not who we were looking for. Instead, we found air traffic controllers, grocery store clerks, funeral directors, minor-league hockey coaches, local meteorologists, First Nations elders, high-rise window washers, and a host of others. These are not the people you see on billboards or featured in interviews—these are your neighbours and members of your community. They are the woman who lives down your street, the guy gassing up at the next pump, and the person you pass by in the airport when you're travelling the country. They are the people who do their jobs in a uniquely Canadian way that makes Canada not only work but thrive. And we can learn from the way they approach their jobs with grace, kindness, and selflessness.

That's what we hope to show in these stories. We also hope that these stories remind you of your own job and how what *you* do, whether it be big or small, contributes to this country.

We are, after all, the sum of our parts.

*Peter Mansbridge*
*Stratford, Ontario*

*The Neskantaga First Nation is hundreds of miles north of Thunder Bay, not far south of James Bay. It is remote, almost hidden among the gorgeous trees, rocky cliffs, lakes, and rivers of northwestern Ontario. It's also home to one of the country's great scandals, a boil-water advisory that dates to the mid-1990s—no other community in modern-day Canada has spent this long without safe drinking water. Its chief is my friend of a few years now, Wayne Moonias.*

---

# THE CHIEF
## Wayne Moonias

I was eleven years old, sitting at my classroom desk, eyes on the old clock on the wall while the snow fell outside. It was November of 1983, and I was very excited because my mother was returning to our home in Neskantaga First Nation that evening. She had been getting health care at the nearest major health centre in Sioux Lookout, a community about 350 kilometres to the southwest. The night before, my father told us that she was bringing back gifts for me and my two younger brothers, Joey and Wilson. When you live in a remote northern community, gifts don't come along very often, and so this news caused quite a stir. I was awake much of the night wondering what she'd gotten for us, and now in class, I couldn't take my eyes off the clock. My mom's Austin Airways plane from Sioux Lookout, with a stop in Sandy Lake First Nation, was due at four p.m., and each minute ticked by at a painfully slow pace.

Finally, the class day was over, and I raced home and waited. Four o'clock came and went, and there was no sign of my mother. Another half hour passed. By five o'clock, my father came home from the airport. Alone. He was clearly distraught.

"Something has happened. I'm not sure what, but it's not good," he said. That was something I didn't want to hear. I was worried.

It had been snowing, heavy at times, that day, but weather in our region is often iffy, and the pilots were used to flying in less-than-ideal conditions to get into Neskantaga First Nation.

"I'm going back to the airport," my father said.

That left me alone in our home. Joey and Wilson were playing down the street with friends. Our home was small, very small. Two bedrooms, one for my parents and one for the three of us boys and our two older siblings, Howard and Dorothy, who were away at high school in Thunder Bay, plus other kids from the community who often stayed with us. My mother called it a "shack" because it was crowded with kids, but she also said it was crowded with love. She was amazing in the way she cared for us and encouraged us, whether it was to play hard or study hard.

But that day, I was alone, sitting and staring at an empty house. Once again, I waited. And waited.

Then my father came home.

"She's gone." For the longest time that was all he said. "She's gone."

I eventually found out that the Twin Otter carrying my mom had been caught in sudden whiteout conditions—snow and freezing rain—moments before it reached the runway. The plane smashed into the ice of a lake about half a mile from the airport. The landing gear was torn off, and the plane spun 180 degrees, slid into the rocks on the shoreline, and then burst into flames. The pilots survived. Four of the five passengers, my mother among them, did not.

My dad was in tears for hours. So were my brothers. And so, too, were all the people who came to our house that evening to grieve. Everyone, that is, except me. I could not cry. I was in shock.

After that day, I became terribly depressed. I started staying away from school. I had once been a bright student with top grades, but now I was failing classes and dropping out. I went from being a kid who had lots of friends to a boy who wanted none. Things got so bad that I considered ending my life.

And then I found a reason to live.

In the weeks and months that followed, my dad's brother, Peter, and his wife, my aunt Maggie, often came by our house to see how we were doing. Uncle Peter was first a councillor and then the chief of our First Nation. His work never stopped, and so I got a front row seat to his job. And it was watching him that helped me out of my depression.

He genuinely cared about people, and he never walked away from someone else's problem. As chief, his phone rang, not just in the daytime, but also in the middle of the night, and he always answered it. The issues were often minor, not that different, except in scale, from what elected officials in urban Canada face, but sometimes they were major, and tragic. A fire, an accident, a missing person in the bush, a child suicide. He was there for them all.

He also dealt with the daily issues facing our community. Everything from managing budgets and securing much-needed jobs in the surrounding Ring of Fire mining district, whose natural resources were and are a great hope for the future, to changing the name of our band from Lansdowne House to its new, more traditional name of Neskantaga First Nation. My uncle also oversaw the relocation of Neskantaga in the late 1980s at the suggestion of the bureaucrats in Ottawa because of infrastructure and flooding issues. It was only about twenty kilometres. Still, moving a community of three hundred people isn't easy, but we did it for the promise of better services, including clean running water in every house.

For decades, the one place we could get safe water was at the local Indian Agent's office because it was the only building that had modern plumbing. After the relocation, in 1993, millions of dollars were spent on the construction of a purification plant, but it was unable to disinfect and deliver clean, safe water to homes. For years, the government has given contract after contract to southern operators to fix the problem, but they have yet to find the solution. In 1995, Neskantaga went under a boil-water advisory. Twenty-eight years later, the advisory is still in place—longer than any other community in Canada. The water crisis continues to plague residents to this day. It's a crisis that is known around the world, and it was the most important issue my uncle faced.

By the time I was in my early twenties, I knew I wanted to be the Uncle Peter of *my* generation. I wanted to confront the problems and try to solve them, so I ran for council. And when, in 2014, Peter was ready to step down, I ran for chief, and here I am—chief of the Neskantaga First Nation. The problems are now mine.

Now, it's me you see when the parade of various federal and provincial officials and documentary film crews from around the world come to Neskantaga. All arrive with their cameras in tow to show their concern for the never-ending boil-water advisories and promise they'll do what they can to end this blight on not only our community, but the province and the country. It's also me who fights for better resources for our schools and medical facilities. It's me who weighs the need for mining jobs against the need to protect our environment. Outsiders don't often realize that, for us, the health of our sturgeon and moose, and the free-flowing nature of our rivers and lakes, is more important than a new mine, even when that mine offers jobs and a more secure financial future for some of our residents.

And it's my phone that rings at three in the morning when a weeping mother tells me her teenage son or daughter, driven by hopelessness for the future, has hung themselves in their room. It's me who goes to the home to help bring the child down. It's me who stays and tries to comfort a family torn by grief. In those times, I often think of Uncle Peter and how he sacrificed to help others. When I was going through *my* grief, he and many others in the community gave up their personal time to do such a mission, and that made so much of a difference in my life—it helped pull me through those terribly dark times. And that's why, now, I try to be the one who shows compassion, who helps bring someone else to the other side of grief.

Out of all the challenges our community faces, it's the ongoing battle for safe water that remains the number one issue. Many of our people complain about scars and sores, and some even say they can't

*As chief of the Neskantaga First Nation, I
work to protect its land and its people.*

take a shower without vomiting. We've been looking for the answer for almost thirty years, and we won't give up until we find it. It's a long list of concerns, and I spend most of my time ensuring that I deal with them and showing that I care about each and every one of our residents, just as my uncle Peter did.

My leadership philosophy is pretty simple. I don't lead from the top down because I don't consider myself at the top. I see myself at the same level as other members of my First Nation, and as such, my role is to be an equal partner in making the community work. We have enough challenges in Neskantaga; we don't need a bossy chief. We need an understanding one, and that's what I try to be.

The past two summers, the Indigenous Services minister, Patty Haidu, has come to Neskantaga. Usually a visit from a federal cabinet minister means a session in the offices of the First Nation with the chief and some councillors, and if there's time, traditional entertainment before the minister heads back to the airport to fly to her next stop. This time, I decided to shelve the official meeting and instead invite people to meet the minister at the community centre. I asked different groups to think about what they wanted to say to the minister and the government—things that impacted their lives, the good and the bad. And they did.

I was there, but I was watching and listening. That's my kind of leadership. Finding the moment to put other people ahead of me, empowering them, and making sure their voices are heard. I want them to know that their chief cares about them and wants to give *them*, not me, the chance to have their say directly to a minister of the Crown. That's what I am most proud of accomplishing in my time as chief.

The day after the plane crash back in 1983, those working at the scene found a piece of luggage. My mother's name was on it: Bessie Moonias. Somehow the bag was still intact. They gave it to my dad, and he brought it home.

Inside were the gifts Mom had purchased in Sioux Lookout for me and my brothers. There were no names on the packages, so my dad chose which one he thought was meant for which son. The one he decided my mother had picked for me was a squishy foam ball with white, red, and blue colours that made me think of Pepsi-Cola. It sounds a bit silly, but still, I think of it as the Pepsi-Cola ball. I played with it endlessly for years, and when it wore out, I replaced it with a new one, which I cherish to this day because it is my connection to my mom.

A few times each year, I head off up or down the river to hunt and fish. I'm Indigenous, after all. Those desires are in my blood, my soul, a part of my core. We are raised to believe that we have a deep connection to the earth and the water, that being on the land is part of our relationship with the Creator. But even kilometres away, the responsibility of being chief never leaves. We have a system of radio links along the waterways, so I'm never out of reach. It's rare, but sometimes I'll get word of a crisis and head back. Some people say, "Why, Chief? Others can handle it." Yes, they can, but I'm the chief, and I'll ask myself, "What would Uncle Peter do?" Case closed. And I head home.

*I've always had a fascination with aviation. I've spent hours at airports just watching the comings and goings of people and planes. I even worked for an airline for a while before I got into broadcasting. And still, today, whenever I pass by or through an airport, I always glance at the air traffic control tower and wonder, "What really goes on in there?" Meet Amber Doiron.*

◆

# THE AIR TRAFFIC CONTROLLER
## Amber Doiron

"So, what do you do for a living?" my new acquaintance asked.

I was out with a group of friends, most of whom I knew and some I'd just met, and the conversation inevitably turned to work. I could have just answered, "I keep people safe." But that would have been too vague. So instead, I replied, "I work at the airport in traffic control."

"Oh," the person said, "so you're one of those people who waves those red and yellow paddles while the pilot taxis the plane into its assigned gate?"

I shook my head. "Uh, no, that's not what I do."

Don't get me wrong. The men and women who marshal aircraft on the tarmac are important players in the overall operations of the airport. What they do is crucial, even critical, to ensuring a flight starts or ends safely.

My job is a little more technical. I sit in the airport tower of the Halifax International Airport, behind the glass walls that overlook the airport runways below. In front of me is a bank of seven monitors with various information about weather, air traffic, and more. At any one time, there could be as many as three or four commercial planes coming in to land, and another four or more lined up ready to depart. The incoming planes are flying at 300 nautical miles an hour, approaching sometimes in different directions and always at different altitudes. And then there are much smaller aircraft, hobby fliers in small one-engine planes and float aircraft moving from one lake to another and often passing over or near the Halifax airport. And helicopters, there are often a few of them in the vicinity as well. As an air traffic controller, it's my job to communicate precise instructions to all the pilots so they can land or take off without incident; if there's a potential conflict, I have anywhere from three to ten seconds to react to keep the hundreds of people on board each of those planes safe. It's an intense job, but I love it.

Growing up in Moncton, New Brunswick, I didn't dream of being an air traffic controller. But I always loved pressure and enjoyed a lot of extreme sports like white water rafting, ocean kayaking, and triathlons. Risk didn't bother me. In fact, the greater the pressure, the calmer I felt. After getting my degree in psychology at the University of New Brunswick, I really wasn't sure what I wanted to do. I tried a few things, but nothing offered the challenge and fulfillment I was looking for.

Then one day, I was listening to one of our neighbours talk about his job as an air traffic controller for NAV Canada. NAV Canada is a not-for-profit corporation that manages the 18 million square kilometres of Canadian civil airspace—one of the largest regions of airspace in the world—and has stations from coast to coast to coast. Our neighbour, a close family friend who had often watched his kids and me playing soccer, worked at the Moncton air traffic tower. As he was describing the high-pressure environment, he said, "Amber, you are great at soccer because you always have your head up and you know where all the players are on the field, so you'd be great at air traffic control."

I thought, "Yes, that's what I want." I begged for a tour of the Moncton tower. Visits aren't normally allowed, but somehow, I was let in. It only took me a few moments to get hooked on the atmosphere, the tension, and all the monitors. I had just seen a glimpse of my future. But looking is easy, doing is a whole different matter.

I filled out the lengthy application for employment form on NAV Canada's website, hoping it would be the only significant hurdle. Wrong. The process for becoming an air traffic controller is very involved and the cut rate is high—and for good reason: thousands, sometimes tens of thousands of lives, depend on the decisions made by controllers every minute of every day in control towers across the country. In other words, the stakes are high. For every hundred people who start the process, after being approved with that initial online application, only about half end up graduating with a controller's licence.

Once I passed muster with the online application, I had a phone interview with a retired controller, then an in-person interview with a panel of NAV Canada employees. All this before I'd been taught anything about air traffic control. What were they looking for in a candidate? That magic mix of ingredients that a controller needs to handle the job—intelligence, decisiveness, and calmness under pressure. I made it through the preliminary cut and was on to the classroom training, where I finally learned what those monitors I saw on my visit to the Moncton tower were for.

The individual monitors provide a series of snapshots that together help the air traffic controller get a full picture of everything that's going on in the airport vicinity, both on the ground and in the air. On the far left is the lighting panel, which controls runway lights, edge lights, guard lights, approach lights, and landing lights. As an air traffic controller, it would be my job to adjust the lighting depending on the time of day and the weather. So if it was foggy, the lighting had to be turned up. The next two screens are the ground radar, which shows all the vehicles, both surface and air, moving around the airport on the ground, and the radar screen, which shows all the airborne aircraft in and around the airport.

Below these three monitors is what's called the integrated working position; in other words, the software used to manage all flight data. The next screen is the long-distance radar and the automated terminal information system, which sends pilots updates about the airport and the weather. Then there's the communications panel with radio frequencies and hotlines to other air traffic control units; when an aircraft leaves the airport's airspace, it's the air traffic controller's job to hand it off to the unit beyond. The last panel is the weather screen with information on everything from wind strength and direction to temperature readings.

As I was finding out, those seven screens contained a vast amount of information, and I had to track each one at all times. Talk about pressure, but I was eager for the challenge.

In training, we were given simulations of air traffic and tested on our ability to take in the information on the screens and make quick decisions on how to direct traffic. The instructors constantly added to the load on our monitors to see how much we could handle and how we avoided potential conflicts. They watched for who panicked, who focused, who dug deep and found solutions, and who was able to juggle a number of other decisions at once and prioritize while not buckling under the pressure.

For me, it really came down to my spatial abilities. It was exactly like what our neighbour had said about my soccer abilities—I could scan all the monitors at once, just like I could see where all the other players were on the field. It was that quality that helped me get my licence, and the job I'd wanted since that day in the Moncton tower when I witnessed it all play out in front of me.

It wasn't long after I became an air traffic controller that those spatial abilities were tested in real time. I was working out of the Halifax International Airport. It was late afternoon, and the weather was closing in a bit—the clouds were low but not so low that pilots would be restricted by their own rules from landing or taking off. Everyone, in the air and in the tower, was monitoring the weather indicators, prepared to adapt if necessary.

It was busy. A lineup of planes was positioned to take off, and another lineup was stacked at different altitudes and coming down to land. And in the tower, I was in the hot seat, directing the traffic to ensure there was enough space between takeoffs and landings to keep everyone safe. There are four runways in Halifax, two at ten thousand feet, two at just under seventy-five hundred feet. And here's a fun fact:

*Here I am in front of the air traffic control tower
at the Halifax Stanfield International Airport.*

the runways a plane uses depend on wind conditions but also on a plane's weight. Once a week, a huge jumbo jet, a 747, comes in empty from South Korea and lands on the shorter runway, but when it leaves, it needs the longer runway, every foot of it, because it's much heavier. Why? It's loaded, and I mean *loaded*, with Nova Scotia's finest—lobster!

On this day, a landing passenger plane was descending through cloud and would soon reach the "final approach" point with the runway straight ahead and ready to receive clearance from the controller, me, to land. Meanwhile, a plane that was prepared to take off was ready to head along the last piece of taxiway to its position at the end of the active runway.

I did my calculations, as I'd been trained to do, in a couple of seconds. Convinced the takeoff plane would have lots of time to lift off and exit the runway area before the landing plane would touch down at the other end of the same ten-thousand-foot runway, I gave him the clearance to head toward the runway for takeoff.

With weather conditions changing, I had a sudden feeling of doubt about how much space there was going to be between the two aircraft. The weather had certainly complicated the equation. There was no room for error. I had to change the plan. I could order the landing plane to abort and "go around"—go full throttle and head back up to altitude and start the whole landing process over again. It's a perfectly safe, heavily practiced manoeuvre for all pilots, but it's no fun for passengers. Within seconds, I made the decision to let the descending aircraft land, and instead I called on the takeoff plane to hold behind the final line marked on the taxiway before entering the runway. But he had already started to move toward the runway on my earlier call. Suddenly, I heard him say: "My nose is over the line."

Now, those lines are about five hundred feet away from the runway, so he wasn't in danger. Still, no pilot wants to be in or seen to be in that position.

Everything went fine. The first plane landed with no issues. The second plane took off without incident a minute later.

But I knew I had initially misjudged things, even though I had recovered quickly and correctly. It wouldn't even qualify as a "close call," but the system is there to ensure safety. Part of that system is Transport Canada regularly going through the communication records between the tower and the various aircraft it's monitoring. Air traffic control is responsible for maintaining minimum distances between aircraft in its zone, and if Transport Canada uncovers something in the recordings that wasn't reported, there will be problems. So to be sure, I reported exactly what happened. No further action was taken.

People often ask me how controllers handle that pressure on a regular basis. Eight hours straight of that would surely send a lot of people to the brink, and that's why we don't do eight hours straight. Not even close. We build in frequent downtime. On a typical day, I spend the first hour and a half in the ground control area monitoring and coordinating all movements on the airport grounds. Then I take a forty-five-minute break to unwind. Then it's into the tower with the seven screens for the next ninety minutes. And then another forty-five-minute break. I keep rotating on that schedule with some occasional differences. By the end of the day's shift, I am tired, borderline exhausted. But again, I love it, and I wouldn't trade it for anything.

When I tell people about my job, I often describe my responsibility as choreography because what goes on in the air and on the ground as aircraft come in for landings and others take off for destinations around the country and the world is a delicate dance. But there are far more partners in this bit of choreography than those like me in the tower and the pilots in the cockpit. The mechanics, the gate agents, the ground crew, the baggage handlers, the flight attendants, the airport administrators, and yes, those men and women with the paddles—we all have our dance steps. And even though it isn't easy, we all make it *look* that way. We make it work.

*So you think your job is challenging? Spare a moment for Craig Houghton. He's the principal of the Fort St. James Secondary School in north central British Columbia. His is no easy job. But just like school principals in big cities and small towns across the country, Craig helps make the country work by leading a team that fosters the next generation.*

---

# THE PRINCIPAL
## Craig Houghton

When you're the high school principal in a small town, you become a community leader by default. That's because the school isn't just a school. It's a gathering place for the community.

Situated on Stuart Lake, our town of Fort St. James is a former fur trading post about a two-hour drive northwest of Prince George, British Columbia. Many of the more than 1,300 people who call this place home work at one of the major sawmills in the area, and their kids attend our school, Fort St. James Secondary School, which has also

become the rec centre for the community. It's hosted wedding receptions and even funerals too. And when we have wildfires in the area—
which is often in north central BC—the school becomes a haven for
people who are forced from their homes. So I'm here working all the
time. I've got to be.

Fortunately, I know my way around these halls because I was once
a student here myself. My father also taught at this school for many
years. I knew I wanted to be a teacher too, so after I studied at the University of Victoria for six years, I came back to northern BC to teach at
Eugene Joseph, an on-reserve, band-operated elementary school serving the Tl'azt'en First Nation community. Later, I returned to Fort St.
James Secondary as a teacher, and then in 2013, I was made principal.

At that time, the school had a low ranking in the province according to the Fraser Institute, a nonpartisan research organization. But
they're looking at straight academics, and while those are important, I
look at a number of other factors. One being the resources available to
us as a small school. And two being the individual student's progress
when it comes to engaging with their studies and their peers.

In a small school, the timetable reflects what we value most. There
are only so many minutes to work with. There are only a certain number of teachers, and they have certain talents. For example, I may want
to have a music program, and the parent advisory committee may want
a music program, but if I don't have a music teacher or the money to
hire one, then we have to focus our efforts elsewhere. For the size of
our school, we have a phenomenal athletic program because we have
a passionate athletic teacher who's really good at motivating students.
About 44 percent of our kids are directly involved in school sports, and
on top of that, we have more kids involved in refereeing or scorekeep-
ing and those kinds of things.

That's the nature of a small school. We can't be great at everything, but we can be great at certain things.

As the principal, I try to be as innovative as possible, and while academics are important, I support programs that prepare our students to contribute in a meaningful way to day-to-day life in BC. For example, we have a small sawmill at the school, and we get wood for the students to cut and make things with. We also have a metal shop and an automotive shop. We have a firefighting program too, where students can train at our local fire hall and go out on real calls. I've seen cases where three people have gone to a house fire. One is an adult and the other two are my grade-11 students.

We also have a grade-12 class that combines environmental studies and geography, where the kids do a lot of learning on the land at a research centre about half an hour away. The centre partners with one of the local First Nations and the University of Northern British Columbia and allows our students to work with professors who may be researching hummingbirds or pine martens, giving them an incredible opportunity.

When it comes to our students' progress, I take into account where our students are starting from and what they might be facing. For example, around two-thirds of our 270 students come from one of the four First Nations located along the lake, and I work very closely with the bands to ensure that we're providing Indigenous kids with the same opportunities as all the other kids.

In speaking with the bands, I've heard firsthand how the parents want their kids to do well. Some have had bad experiences in public school themselves, and as a result, aren't necessarily able to tell their kids what it takes to be successful academically. Others may be dealing with substance abuse or in and out of jail. Many of our kids are being raised by grandparents who may have survived a residential school, and so sometimes, the grandparents are nervous about coming to our school. I'm not a big man—I'm 5' 6"—but I recognize that as a white guy with a tie, I might make them uncomfortable. I do my best to address that. What I've learned is that when grandparents come in, I need to listen. They are there to talk about their grandchild, but often they get to talking about their own lives, and I'm humbled by what they have endured. Their grandkid may be acting out or falling behind, and the teachers may be at their wits' end, but when I hear what the family is going through and how they are trying to help their grandchild, I feel for them.

And then I try to come up with a very specific plan for that student, whether that's seeing a counsellor or making a homework schedule. I might say, "Block one is math. Block two is history. And so on." In two weeks, we can go over what's been happening, hour by hour. It's a good exercise for everyone to see how the student's time is spent. Do they need more sleep? Do they need to block off more time for homework? And how can the school and the family work together to make those things happen?

These are the cultural nuances that we need to be mindful of if we're to truly bring about reconciliation. Because the federal government funds education for Indigenous kids who live on reserves, the bands contract us to teach those children. Given the historic relationship between government educators and Indigenous communities, the bands are very watchful. They want to make sure there's no systemic racism. They want to make sure their kids are being treated equally. And they're right to have these concerns.

There's no doubt in my mind that twenty-five years ago, we had systemic racism at the school. I know that for a fact. I was part of it.

I was part of the system. But now I'm part of the system to change things for the better. Reconciliation isn't just a word. It's action.

Take, for example, our senior girls' soccer team. After we have try-outs for the team, I look at who made the team and who didn't. And I ask, do we have a fair representation of First Nations and non–First Nations? And if we don't, I ask why. I want to be sure we're giving everyone a fair chance to succeed.

The First Nations community has been vocal and said, "That's not okay anymore." And it isn't. So, we're making progress. The town is changing, the province is changing, and the country is changing with regard to how we treat First Nations people. For me, that starts at our school, and it starts by meeting the students where they're at.

We do our absolute best to hire as many Indigenous people as possible at the school. We have only one First Nations certified teacher, but we also have learning-support workers from the community to assist the teachers. And we have a great system of bringing in knowledge holders, elders, and hereditary chiefs to work with our kids.

The hardest part of my job is trying to motivate our students. We see kids who are playing video games or watching Netflix all night. In the morning, they get on the school bus, and they arrive at school exhausted. We also have children from very traumatic homes, who find it hard to come to school and get excited about it. When that happens, we let them go to what we call our calming room, where there are some couches and food. We don't ask why they're there; we just invite them to sit, release some anxiety, get themselves together before they go to class.

One of our youth workers created a critical food program so every person in the school gets free breakfast every day, and if they need it, a free lunch too. Any time during the day, they can get bagels, toast, cheese, and a variety of fruit. That's part of our caring process and how we help the kids in our community.

And I think the students understand we're here to protect them because they protect the school. Fort St. James has some crime, but we have almost no vandalism at school. Sometimes a student will have a bit of a temper tantrum and punch a window or a wall, but generally in the summer and on the weekends, this place is not targeted.

So what the Fraser Institute doesn't see is the gains that the kids have made from grade 8 to grade 12. They don't see the kid who arrives here with his hoodie over his head and is afraid to look at you. Or the kid who has substance abuse issues. Or the unfortunate fetal alcohol spectrum disorder. Or those with learning disabilities. They don't see that. They don't see the poverty, the intergenerational trauma, the isolation. When a student has all that working against them, we can't pretend they're like every other student in the province. But it doesn't mean they can't be successful in life.

We're never going to be like every other high school in the province. That's just the way it is. We can't have stuck-in-the-box thinking. We can't be thinking that Vancouver does something one way, so we have to do it the same way. No, we have to meet the needs of the kids in front of us. Sometimes, that means going back to the basics. Because we can't teach fractions to someone who doesn't know their times tables. We have to build that knowledge in them so that when they reach grade 12, they can graduate with a legitimate diploma they've earned and the skills to do well.

Which is why every graduate is a success story for us, and really for everyone in town. Our graduation ceremony is important. It's a community weekend celebration. We have a formal ceremony in the gym on Friday night, where the grads walk up in their caps and gowns

*Here I am with Javon Felix, one of our 2023 shop class students who loves woodworking, in front of our school sign, which was made by a group of our students.*

and get their diplomas. Then on Saturday, they dress up in nice clothes and parade through the town. Everyone comes out to see them. Fort St. James comes to a standstill because it's grad weekend.

We're proud that almost everyone does graduate. We find that many of our students take six years instead of the standard five years, but then 95 percent of all our students earn a diploma.

Over the years, we have had some wonderful success stories. Two years ago, we had a First Nations kid from one of the outlying communities who loved to play basketball. He had family support, but not what you would see in a larger town or city, where a parent can drive him around and pay for him to be in tournaments. This kid found a place to stay in town so he wouldn't have to ride the school bus every day and could play basketball. He worked hard, became the class valedictorian, and went off to a college in Manitoba.

But the reality is, sometimes the kids break your heart. We work so hard with these kids, and we think they're excelling, and then in a year or two later, we might see one downtown asking for money, sometimes drunk or under the influence. That's hard. Because I know they have potential. I know they're capable of so much more.

Do I blame myself? Partially, yes. I'm not perfect. I have lots of flaws. But our school is all about opportunity. We try to open doors for kids who have not seen too many open doors. And that's all I can continue to do. Because it's personal for me. I'm part of this community and I know all the kids by name. I've even taught some of the parents. I know most of their families and they know me, so I would never go to a larger centre because this is my home, and I want to do what I can to make it a better place.

*Most of us love hockey. We're Canadian after all. And hundreds of thousands of young Canadian boys and girls play organized hockey. Their skills and their minds, too, are molded by coaches. Important life values are often set at a young age by coaches, and the good ones believe that while winning is the goal, so is becoming responsible Canadians. The Peterborough Petes have developed a record number of NHL players. Their coach is Rob Wilson.*

---

# THE HOCKEY COACH
## Rob Wilson

I'm a hockey nerd. Always have been. As a kid, everything in my room was hockey, from my bedspread, which featured all the NHL team logos, to the matching curtains. I grew up in Toronto, and I absolutely loved the Leafs. I knew every statistic and every player. There wasn't anything I didn't know about that team. From a young age, I wanted hockey to be my life.

Today, as the coach of the Peterborough Petes, I'm living the life I always wanted.

Most hockey fans see me only during the games. I'm the guy behind the bench doing a lot of pacing. But by the time the game starts, I've already been at work for twelve hours.

I get to the rink around seven a.m., and so do the assistant coaches. We usually check a short video of game footage from the team we'll be playing that night, make sure it's just right for what we want to show the players later. We'll talk about our game plan. There might be some one-on-one meetings with players, a meeting with each of the four lines, maybe even a team meeting.

Then, at 9:30, we have our pregame skate. Everyone is on the ice. After that, we have our video session.

At about 2:30, the players who aren't in the lineup that night have another on-ice practice.

At five o'clock, we have a short meeting with the guys who will be on the power play and another short meeting with the penalty-killing units. At 5:20 on the dot, we have a full team meeting.

Once all the prep is done, I try to relax, have a coffee or a quick bite to eat. I'll check the lineups, maybe watch the warmups before game time.

During the game, part of my job is to motivate. I remind everyone of their responsibilities on the ice, and I watch how the other coach is matching his lines against ours.

One of our assistant coaches stays near me and communicates with a coach watching the game from higher up in the arena, who lets us know what he's seeing. The assistant coach is also linked to our video room, so I might see something on the ice and turn to him to say,

"Mark that clip. I didn't like our backchecking there." Or "How did we miss our assignment on that play?"

The video coach will have the clips ready for me during the intermission. I'll go right to him, look at the seven or so clips I wanted, but I'll pick just two or three to show the players because I don't want to overload them. Then I go into the dressing room and say, "Okay, this is what's happening. Look how we're running around in the defensive zone. They're beating us and getting pucks to the net." And then another clip. "We're not entering the offensive zone effectively. We've got to be better on the rush."

I'm intense, but I don't yell. I try to be respectful. I try not to embarrass or belittle anybody because I don't think that works. As a coach, it's my job to give constructive criticism, to tell them what they're doing and how they can do it better. And I never go to the media and call out an individual player who may have made a mistake. That's for us to talk about as a group. Then we go back out to finish the game—win or lose.

That's the technical side of what I do, but coaching is so much more than that. As American basketball coach John R. Wooden said, "A good coach can change a game. A great coach can change a life." And I know that to be true from my own experience . . .

I made it to the Ontario Hockey League, playing for the Sudbury Wolves, and when I was eighteen, I was drafted by the Pittsburgh Penguins. The next fall, I went to the NHL training camp, where I was in awe of some of the players on the ice. Just a couple of years earlier, I'd been in my basement with my dad watching them on TV, and now I was sharing the ice with them. Maybe I was a little too starstruck, because at the camp I remember thinking, "Oh, there's Mario

Lemieux," when maybe I should have been a little more focused on me. Yes, Mario Lemieux was on the ice, but so was I. I should have realized that meant I was pretty good too.

In reality, though, there was no way I was making that team. Maybe a first-round draft pick had a shot, but I was selected in round twelve of the draft, number 235 overall. In any case, I was a little too immature. I didn't make it past the training camp and onto the roster, and even though I was expecting that, it still hurt. I wasn't about to give up, though. I was determined to play, and to make my living at it.

Easier said than done.

After the training camp, I went back to the OHL, playing two more seasons with the Wolves, then I was traded to the Peterborough Petes. Peterborough was a great hockey town, as I soon found out. Everyone got behind the Petes; it was as if we were the Maple Leafs of Toronto—they made us players feel important and supported. Peterborough was much closer to my home in Toronto. Instead of driving more than four hours to watch me play in Sudbury, my parents now had a quick ninety-minute trip to Peterborough. Even my older brother was able to come, so I felt supported on all fronts.

While we weren't the best team in the league that year, the entire town was behind us. And we came together and played really well when it mattered most, and we ended up going all the way in the OHL playoffs and winning the championship. The J. Ross Robertson Cup wasn't the Stanley Cup, but for a kid who dreamed of hoisting a championship trophy over his head, winning it was the greatest moment of my life to that point.

And it was the best way to close out my career as a junior.

Back home in Toronto, I talked with my parents about the future. It was clear I would never play in the NHL, so I was at a crossroads.

PETERBOROUGH PETES HOCKEY CLUB 1988-89

*Photo Courtesy: Peterborough Petes*

*The team photo from my year playing for the Peterborough Petes. I'm in
the back row, fifth from the left, with #25 just visible on my arm.*

It was time to make a decision about the rest of my life. My mom was a huge advocate for education, and she tried to get me to think about going to university, but I had no interest. Academics just weren't my thing. In my gut, I knew I wanted to be in hockey.

So for the next couple of years, I bounced around the American Hockey League and the East Coast Hockey League, but that wasn't working out well. I was pretty disappointed in myself, like I had underachieved, and I began to doubt whether I was a strong player. I even started to think about a career as a police officer or a firefighter.

Then, one day, the phone rang. It was Tom Barrett, who had coached in the OHL and was now coaching the Chatham Wheels, a new minor-league team in Chatham, Ontario. He asked me to come play for him. I'll never forget what he said.

"So your path hasn't worked the way you wanted it to," he said to me. "But it doesn't mean you're not a really good hockey player. It doesn't mean that you don't have value as a hockey player. You're not in the NHL, but don't beat yourself up over it, it's not the end of the world. There's still a lot of hockey left in you."

His words made me rethink what hockey meant to me. I said yes to Tom's offer and headed to Chatham. Tom was what we call "a player's coach." He was a good communicator, one who was old school enough to make you know when you weren't doing something right, but always careful to make you feel good about yourself. Under Tom's coaching, I regained confidence in my abilities. I saw that success in hockey didn't have to mean playing in the NHL. I realized very few people ended up doing that, but there were other ways to make my dream come true and make a living in hockey. That was probably when coaching first entered my mind, but only for down the road. My time in Chatham resurrected my fire for the game. I forgot about becoming a police officer or firefighter and focused on being a good athlete and team player.

Then I was offered the chance to play in England for the Steelers, a new club in Sheffield (about 250 kilometres northwest of London) that was getting big crowds of up to 10,000 people, and it was paying pretty good money. My parents were from the UK, so I always felt a little British, and I had actually played a few games in Britain five years earlier, so it was easy to accept the offer. I made the move, which I never regretted.

Two years in, I started to consider what I was going to do when my playing days were over. I knew I wanted to stay in the game and be hands-on. Coaching seemed like the best option. I thought I'd have fun trying to figure out ways to win games from behind the bench, and it would be satisfying to help young men improve their skills. So, when I came home from England in the summers, I took coaching lessons from Hockey Canada. I listened to lectures, wrote exams, went to coaching clinics, and slowly I became accredited to coach at higher and higher levels. I coached in Britain and then in Italy and Germany.

During that time, I kept in touch with a couple of people I knew who were on the board of directors of the Peterborough Petes. We talked about whether I'd ever consider coming back to Canada to coach, but there was nothing concrete about it. The Petes had a bad year in 2017, and suddenly the talk about coming home became more serious. It was a big decision. I loved coaching in Europe, and I was good at it. I won way more games than I lost, and I was even named Coach of the Year in 2017. But in my heart I wanted to come back to Canada, and the offer from the Petes was very tempting. After all, playing for the Petes and winning the championship was one of the best times in my hockey career. It had been a privilege to play there.

It would be a privilege to coach there too. I would be following in the footsteps of hockey royalty, including Scotty Bowman, who went on to become the winningest coach in NHL history; Roger Neilson, known as one of the most innovative coaches ever; Gary Green, who became the youngest coach in NHL history; and Mike Keenan, another Stanley Cup winner.

The Petes have produced more NHL players than any other junior team in the world, so when I started with them in 2018, my job was—and still is—to develop the players into the best hockey players they can be. Every player in the OHL is among the very best junior players in the world. Every one of them has worked hard to make it this far, and of course they want to make it all the way to the NHL. It makes it easier to coach them because they have that desire to be the best they can be. My job is to encourage them, one-on-one and as a group, assuring them that they have what it takes, and to point out what may be the small things that separate those who make it from those who don't.

That's what I focused on in my first season with the Petes—growing the talent and winning as many games as we could. Winning isn't everything, but it does build morale and team spirit. And it helps the players develop. Winning teams make the playoffs, which exposes them to a new atmosphere. And the more rounds a team wins, the more games they play in front of scouts, which is so important to a hockey player's career. A losing team just doesn't get as much ice time, and the scouts are more likely to forget those players when they start to see other guys.

As a coach in junior hockey, I knew that my role was more than developing hockey players—it was also developing young men. There was no question that the players on the Petes were talented, high-level athletes, but as I got to know them, I was reminded that they were also just boys. Some of them were away from home for the first time and came from families with different backgrounds and cultures, which I had to be aware of. Along with my assistant coaches, we made sure to talk to each player every day they were away from home. We got to know the names of their siblings and their parents and established a connection. The older ones, around twenty years old, had been in the league for four years, and they needed different kinds of support. Right from the beginning, I knew I had to make sure each of my play-ers felt supported and help guide them to make good choices, not just during the game, but before and after—and outside the arena.

That first season (and every season after), I made sure to tell my players that they represent Peterborough, and as such, they have a re-sponsibility to be good role models, not just when they're doing school visits but whenever they're out. They may be only sixteen or seventeen years old, but young kids look up to them like they're Auston Matthews. When the team had an away game and we went to a restaurant for a meal, I made sure everyone took their hat off at the table. Little things like no baseball caps during meals reminded the players that it's important to be professional, and that they're in the public eye.

That's been my approach since 2018. After that first season, COVID-19 arrived. It cut short the following season, when I thought we had a real chance to win, and then it cancelled the next season entirely. I literally cried. It was really tough on all of us. The players and coaches, of course, but I also recognize how hard it was on others—the people selling Coke and hot dogs at the rink, our bus drivers, even the stick boys. Maybe we all learned that we shouldn't take the things we enjoy in life for granted. Then in 2023, the team made a run at the championship title. The city came together to cheer us on. As we won round after round in the playoffs, it was all people could talk about.

And then, we won.

Thirty-four years after I had raised the J. Ross Robertson trophy over my head as a Petes player, I did it again as the team's coach. The win felt incredible. And it was a joy to feel the community spirit that was behind us as we headed into the Canadian Hockey League championship. That didn't go as well as we had hoped. We finished third, but no one thought of us as losers. I couldn't walk into a store without someone saying to me, "Well done, Coach." Or "That was a great run, Coach." It would be the same in North Bay or Owen Sound or Flin Flon. In my five years coaching the Petes, I've come to appreciate that hockey, especially junior hockey, is the heart and soul of so many communities.

When the hockey season ends, my job doesn't. I try to get some downtime. It usually takes me three to four weeks to shake off the tensions of the season and begin to relax. But then it's time to gear up for the next season. I have to work with our general manager and our scouts to see which players we'll draft from both North America and Europe. I'm on the phone. I'm watching video.

And when the NHL draft happens in the summer, I'll get calls from NHL teams asking questions about the players I've coached. How do I see them as professionals? My role is to help promote my guys, but I always tell the truth. I share all the good things, but I have to talk about the not-so-good things as well.

The hardest part of coaching is telling somebody that their dream is over, that they're not going to make the team, or they're not going to be invited back the next season. Losing is a hard part of the game,

*Two of my players were drafted in the second round of the 2019 NHL draft. On the left is Hunter Jones, who was selected by the Minnesota Wild, and on the right is Nick Robertson, who was picked by the Toronto Maple Leafs.*

but giving bad news to my players is worse. They've put their hearts and souls into hockey their whole lives. I know firsthand what that disappointment feels like, and I've always felt the kindest approach is to be direct and upfront. It still doesn't feel good, but I hope I can use my experience to show them that it doesn't mean hockey can't be part of their lives.

I still have close relationships with a lot of the guys I've coached over the last twenty years, so I think I've treated them right. Many call me many years later and say, "Thanks for everything you did for me. I didn't realize back then that you were teaching me important things I'd always remember." That's when I think of Wooden's quote about what a great coach can do. I have it on a sign behind my desk now.

I feel very fortunate that I've been able to make a living in hockey my whole life, especially since there's not a lot of job security in the game, particularly for coaches. I've heard that in baseball, where they play 162 games a year, a great coach might be able to win just a handful of games with his strategy or teaching, six or seven games tops. Hockey is a completely different sport, and I wouldn't even be able to give you a guess as to how many games a good coach can win. All I'd say is that it's more than zero. A coach has a big influence in my opinion. But a coach can't win without good players.

If coaches have a couple of bad weeks, the rumours swirl that they'll be fired, the fans start to chant their name, and suddenly they're gone. It happened to me once in Europe. It's just part of the game. It hurts. But you have to have thick skin, pick yourself up, and move on. That's what I did all those years ago when I didn't make it past that NHL training camp. And I'm still in the game today because that's what it's about for me. So, I'm just going to keep coaching as long as I can.

*Mark and I are old enough to remember when Percy Saltzman used to throw a piece of chalk in the air to signal the end of his nightly weather forecast, on what was then black-and-white television. Percy was a rock star of early Canadian TV—the first weatherperson viewers knew on the tube. Everyone loved Percy, even when he was wrong, which, back in the fifties and sixties, was certainly more frequent than the high-tech meteorologists of today, like Christy Climenhaga, who tells weather stories to the people of Alberta and Saskatchewan.*

◆

# THE METEOROLOGIST
## Christy Climenhaga

When I was ten years old, my father began a new hobby. He, a real-life renaissance man, learned to fly. I was so excited. I couldn't wait until he started touring the skies over Central Alberta with me at his side. It started with him teaching me about the importance of the "walk-around," those few minutes where a pilot, any pilot, even the ones flying the huge jumbo jets (or "heavies" as the pilots call them) that carry hundreds of passengers, slowly walk around the plane, checking every spot to ensure that things are in the right position and that there are no serious scratches, dents, or leaks—nothing that could cause even the slightest concern. My family still has pictures of me as a little girl with my dad doing the walk-around for one of the single-engine planes my dad first flew.

But for me, the serious thrills weren't on the ground; they were in the air, and within a few years, I earned the right to enjoy them by sitting—unofficially, of course—in the right-hand seat. There were even times when I was still barely old enough to peer over the dashboard of instruments in front of me that Dad would let me take control for a few seconds. When I could see over that barrier, I was blown away by the scenery, especially the huge swaths of prairie farmland stretching out to the foothills and the puffy white clouds that would accumulate across the skies. Sometimes by mid-afternoon on hot summer days, the clouds would turn dark, and I'd hear my father say, "We have to stay away from those." With warnings like that, it didn't take long for me to realize that it's one thing to understand and manage the mechanics of flying, but it's quite another to understand and manage the mechanics of weather. And if there's one thing pilots will tell you, it's that if you don't understand the impact of weather on flying, and how to manage it, your flying days are going to be a challenge, maybe worse.

That's how I became fascinated by weather, or "atmospheric science" as the academics call it. And while I kept flying as a hobby after getting my own licence at nineteen, I knew I wanted weather as my career. So, it was off to the University of Alberta to get a degree in atmospheric sciences. The program was an intense four years. I began with general credits like physics and biology and chemistry and then started specializing in the earth sciences and doing atmospheric modeling. Now, when I look back at my fourth-year notes, there was not a single English word there—it's all formulas and Latin letters, evidence of just how specialized and complicated understanding weather can be.

It was hard, but I loved it. Partly because I love science. I always wanted to know more about the impact of weather systems on the land, on the crops, on us. So many things are connected, and I knew if I could grasp it, I could explain it, and I could make people's lives that much better by passing the knowledge along. Most of that knowledge came in the classroom, but some came through real life experience.

During my second year at university, I took one of my final flight exams. I was flying solo doing "circuits and bumps," a simple and straightforward procedure where I flew in a rectangle alongside the active runway at the airport. On the final leg of the rectangle (that's the circuit) I descended to touch down (that's the bump), then sped up to take off again. I repeated the exercise again and again. While I was focusing on my takeoffs and landings, something else was happening that caught me a bit off guard. The wind was picking up, and each time I came in to land, it was just a bit stronger. By my last touchdown, I was fighting a crosswind like I hadn't experienced before. To deal with it, I was flying almost perpendicular to the runway itself, just to be able to slip down enough.

When I taxied to the hangar and saw my instructor, she looked at me, unsmiling, and said, "It was getting a little dicey out there. It was time to come down."

She was right. I had been studying weather phenomenon at school, and I remember thinking, "Wow, I really should have known better at this point." That experience taught me in real terms, not just the textbook terms, how powerful the weather can be and how it can change quickly, and at times, wildly.

After graduation, I got a CBC scholarship to go to Toronto and train in broadcasting with special emphasis on weather. One of the courses I took involved a casual lecture by the CBC's chief correspondent, Peter Mansbridge. I was so nervous that I hid behind others at the back of the room and never asked a question. (Odd, now that ten years later he's writing a book and including *me*!)

A few months later, I was on to my first real assignment, facing real weather head on during a three-year assignment in Yellowknife. Edmonton has rough winter weather, but Yellowknife was a whole new experience. There's something about cold—real cold—that once you feel it, you don't forget it. Nothing prepared me for what it was really like there. That first winter in Yellowknife, the thermometer outside read minus forty-five degrees Celsius, and with the windchill, it was minus fifty-five. I remember walking to my car. I had my snowmobile gear on, but I foolishly hadn't made sure my gloves were on right, and when I touched the doorhandle, it felt like my skin was burning. When I finally got inside the car, it wouldn't start, so I had no choice but to walk almost two kilometres. Even in my snowmobile gear, the cold was a shock to the system.

That day made me realize the full extent of weather's impact on the daily lives of the people in the north. As broadcasters, our news headline and our weather headline were neck and neck in terms of importance. I may have been based in Yellowknife, but I covered a huge area, from Yukon to Northwest Territories to Nunavut, and if I left one small community out of my daily forecast, I knew someone from that community would have an email in my inbox by the time I got back to my desk. And I understood. For example, in a place like Baker

Lake, the blizzard capital of Canada, things can change on a dime, so knowing the weather forecast was essential for the people of Baker Lake to plan their life. It's easy to forget there are thousands, if not tens of thousands, of people living in those huge gaps on the weather map between the major cities, but my time in the north taught me that weather forecasts mean as much to those small communities as they do to big cities. I tried then and I try now to always include some of those communities and give them ample warning of what, good or bad, may be heading their way.

As a meteorologist, I look at a lot of data generated by sophisticated computers that use complex mathematical models to give me an idea of what's happening and what's going to happen, but not all meteorologists agree with the conclusions. Sometimes, I think, "Okay, Environment Canada, I hear what you're suggesting with your forecasts, but let me add my location-specific experience." In other words, if I've seen this kind of weather system before and in my area, I know that it doesn't always go by the traditional weather book. Again, weather forecasts matter. It's not just families planning a picnic who are relying on our forecasts, it's also firefighters engaged with a huge forest fire where a percentage of humidity or a wind shift can make a huge difference to their safety. We live in an age where we can ask our watches what the weather will be like tomorrow, and they will tell us. But there is still a human element. As a meteorologist, I use my experience to forecast the weather path too.

Years later, when I was based in Regina, I remember listening to the radio at home, and I heard the general forecast talking about a system coming in from Alberta that may produce gusty winds. I checked my data and saw the same thing, but I also recalled similar conditions before that set up a situation that turned nasty. I did some calculations, called the station, and said I was coming in, that people needed to be ready. I went to my garage to get my car, but a tree had toppled and fallen directly on the garage, pinning my car underneath. Those winds were already more than gusty. I ended up running to work, dodging trash cans that had blown into the street. It took me fifteen minutes, but I got there, caught my breath, and went on air to advise caution. It wasn't a tornado, but it was a serious wind warning, and I felt I had used my local knowledge to prepare my neighbours for what was happening and what was still coming.

My experience has come in handy on other occasions too. A couple of summers ago, a friend of mine was getting married in an outdoor ceremony, and she was in a panic the morning of the big day because it was raining. She kept looking at me and saying, "Christy, I don't want to walk down the aisle in the rain. When is it going to stop pouring?" The pressure was on. I grabbed my phone and pulled up whatever local weather data I could find, from radar images to forecasts, and started doing my own analyzing. Finally, I looked up at the bride and said, "Delay everything twenty minutes, wait it out, and you should be fine." All that atmospheric science stuff paid off, the twenty minutes did it. That was the highest stress weather forecast I've ever given.

Of course, I'm not always right. Some of the strangers who stop me in the grocery store or on the street will vouch for that. They'll say, almost always good-naturedly, "Hey, Christy, you said it wasn't going to rain, but it did!" Well, no one is perfect, and even with all our resources and experience, the weather can still be unpredictable. But I'd say generally, meteorologists are right at least 75 percent of the time. As someone once said to me, even Connor McDavid doesn't score goals on 75 percent of his shots, Tom Brady doesn't have a 75 percent passing average, and name a baseball player who has ever hit .750. Would we like to be right all the time? Of course. We'll keep working at it.

When the CBC moved me south after my stint in Yellowknife, I went from covering a huge swath of the north to a huge swath of the prairies and western Canada. Some things were the same, like the focus on winter weather and the cold temperatures, even though they were less extreme. The biggest difference was the importance of water and precipitation. For an area with a difficult history of drought, the fear of its return makes farmers shudder. I stood in the fields with farmers to understand that fear. I looked at a pond, once filled with water and now dry, the bottom, parched earth, and I heard their unanswered prayers for rain. I also heard stories about when the rain finally came and how it wasn't enough to change things overnight. I learned that it could take months, if not years, to return to what used to be normal.

I began to realize that those days of normalcy might never come . . .

So I started to focus on climate change, especially at the local level. That's my main job now. Most people accept that climate change is real. The science supports it, and there's no other rational explanation for all the rapid change we're seeing. But there are a few deniers still out there. When I encounter one, I show them the evidence, the temperature tables, the water tables. But I understand that it's such a big topic and can feel dense and inaccessible to many. Some people may simply conclude, "Okay, sea level rise: bad," and leave it at that. But I'm in Alberta, far removed from sea-level issues.

Now, in my broadcasts, I've moved away from daily weather forecasting except in emergencies, and instead I concentrate on telling the story of climate change from a local, almost personal perspective. To find out what changing climactic conditions mean for someone living in Saskatchewan or Alberta and what their life will look like twenty,

*Talking with Robert Grandjambe for a story about how industry and climate change are affecting the water levels in the Peace–Athabasca Delta.*

thirty, even fifty years from now, I talk to scientists, not in their labs, but in the fields, where they're studying the change. They use their specific skills to document their findings, and then I use mine to communicate the results in a way that people will be receptive to and will help them understand what's happening—because what's happening is going to change their lives.

## Postscript

*Christy will be able to read this book at home because that's where she is these days, on maternity leave with her second child.*

*And does she still fly? Oh yes, and it's still something she cherishes to do with her dad, who now owns a vintage 1940s canvas-covered Fleet Canuck. The rest of us, me especially, are jealous!*

*Our justice system is one of the most important aspects that strive to keep our nation fair and just for everyone. At least, that's the way it's supposed to work. As a legal aid lawyer, Margaret Gallagher is an integral part of trying to make the system reach its goal of fairness. Since 2005, she's worked in Saint John with the New Brunswick Legal Aid Services Commission, where she's one of twenty-five criminal lawyers.*

---

# THE LAWYER
## Margaret Gallagher

On almost a daily basis, I hear someone who's been accused of a crime say, "I'm not going to get legal aid, I'm going to get a real lawyer." That's a shame. I'm a full-time legal aid lawyer, and as real as they come. I've tried cases of every kind, argued at appeal courts, and at the Supreme Court of Canada. I've heard many accused people tell a judge, "No, I don't want anything to do with legal aid. I'm going to represent myself" or "I'm going to hire a lawyer."

Then they do, or they don't, or they can't, and they come back to legal aid for help, and of course we do. It's our job.

When I was in grade three, I knew I wanted to be a lawyer. I developed a keen interest in criminal law because of the Stephen Truscott case. He was a fourteen-year-old boy convicted of raping and murdering a female classmate in 1959. It took almost fifty years for the courts to conclude he had been wrongfully convicted. If not for his age, he would have been executed.

At university, I became passionate about legal aid—government-sponsored legal representation for those who cannot afford it. I even wrote a term paper on what I perceived as an abysmal situation in the funding and coverage of legal aid. When I graduated and went into private practice, I was happy to represent legal aid clients, though people advised me not to identify myself as a legal aid lawyer. The system has changed now, and all I do is legal aid, working for the New Brunswick Legal Aid Services Commission.

While most of the people we represent are male, I find more and more women are entering the criminal justice system. Regardless of gender, there is no particular age group that uses legal aid; I've had clients from eighteen to eighty. The common denominator is income. And that's because a person has to be poor to qualify for legal aid. Most of my clients are on social assistance, or they have no income at all.

About half my clients have a mental health issue or an addiction to an illegal substance. Poverty and addiction both fuel crime. If somebody's charged with stealing watches from a store, it's typically to re-sell on the street to feed their addiction. If they've stolen baby formula and diapers, that's a different story that reflects the way society treats people. Maybe they wouldn't be committing crimes if they had better funding from social assistance. I'm not here to advocate for that; I'm just saying it's a reality. People shouldn't have to steal in order to feed themselves or their family. I've had clients who threw a rock through a window in the middle of winter and then waited for the police to come take them to a warm place. That speaks badly of us as a society.

I see a lot of repeat offenders. Sometimes someone gets out on Tuesday and they're back on Thursday. One of the reasons I do what I do is to try to stop that revolving door and prevent our jails from becoming even more crowded than they are now. I think the police sometimes arrest people on insufficient grounds. The incarceration rate is very high for people with mental illness, for Indigenous people, and for people who have previously committed a crime.

The public too often believes that if someone is charged with a crime, they must be guilty. And they don't understand why I defend them. Put simply, I want fairness for them. Whether they are charged with catching undersized lobster, having moose meat in their freezer (seemingly a small crime, but it comes with jail time), theft, insurance fraud, assault, or even murder. Some of the things my clients have done are repugnant. Some of the facts in some cases are awful. But as a lawyer, I have to look beyond that and ensure they get a fair trial, and that justice is properly applied. Which is why I have no trouble representing people who are guilty. (As a rule of thumb, I never ask a client if they're guilty; I just ask them to tell me what happened.)

When it comes to justice, I look for Charter violations, and it's surprising how often I find them. This is sometimes referred to as getting someone off on a "technicality." But my question would be: Why do we have a Charter of Rights and Freedoms if we're going to ignore it?

That Charter is there for each one of us. We all have to believe we have certain rights—the right to not be arrested without cause, the right to a fair and impartial trial. If the most vulnerable in society are deprived of those rights, we can all be deprived of them.

Anyone arrested in Canada has the right to a lawyer. When someone is arrested, the police must tell them that they have a right to a lawyer, and that if they can't afford a lawyer, legal aid is available, and provide the phone number for legal aid. If I'm the duty counsel at legal aid, then I answer that call. It could be in the middle of the day or night.

The first thing I tell every prisoner is what their rights are. For example, if someone is charged with impaired driving, I remind them they have the right to refuse a breathalyzer test, but in all likelihood, they'll be charged with refusal to take a breathalyzer, and that will be much harder to defend—they did refuse on record—than if they were to take, and fail, the test.

Every arrested person is also entitled to a lawyer at their first court appearance. Each morning, a legal aid lawyer from our office talks to the people who are in cells, waiting to appear in court. That could be as many as twenty people. We explain their situation, the process ahead, and represent them at their bail hearing when the Crown objects to a person's release.

As a legal aid lawyer, I have a heavy workload. But I try to make sure every client gets all the attention necessary. I don't think I'm short of time or resources. In some ways, I'm more able to focus on a case than a lawyer from a big law firm who's worried about billable hours to pay the rent.

And I have tried major cases, both in trial and on appeal. In one

*At the Saint John Law Courts.*

case, I argued successfully that a man who had been convicted of murder should be released pending his appeal. The resulting newspaper headline was nasty, and my name was in the story, which sent several ugly messages my way. But eventually, midway through his second trial, the Crown stayed the charges, realizing mistakes had been made.

In another case, I successfully appealed a murder conviction, and at the second trial the Crown accepted a plea of manslaughter, a lesser charge. So instead of a life sentence without parole for at least twenty-five years, my client had already served almost her entire sentence on the lesser charge.

The victim is a very important person in a courtroom. I never lose sight of that. But as a legal aid lawyer, my focus is on the only person whose liberty is at stake, the accused. Which is not to say I get emotionally tied to them. I don't. Sometimes my clients tell people, "She's my lawyer," and they seem to believe I really belong to them. They expect me to call every day, even when we're six months from trial. That just isn't possible. They'll have my full attention when it's needed, but I have to set boundaries.

Still, I understand why they want to lean on me. They're in the most frightening position they'll ever be in, especially if this is the first time they've been charged with a crime. Everything is foreign to them. They don't know where to stand, what to say, what not to say.

I had a woman who was an absolute emotional wreck. She was young, and she had serious mental health issues, and she asked, "Are they going to take me away today?" I assured her that nobody was taking her away. I only do that when I feel reasonably confident, but I can't offer false assurances. If someone has a criminal record four pages long, I can't tell them they're not going to jail. I can't sugarcoat the truth. If somebody has bought a $4,000 computer on the street for $50, it's very hard to argue they're not guilty of possessing stolen property.

"But I didn't know it was stolen," they'll tell me.

I then explain the concept of willful blindness—conscious avoidance of the truth—and say, "Well, you can take the stand and stick to your story, but you're going to face a very aggressive cross-examination, and I think you'll be convicted."

It's often more difficult to deal with the families of the accused. Nobody wants somebody they love to go to jail. I represented two brothers who were in court just a few hours apart. Their mother asked me if one of the cases could be set over for the next week because she said, "I can't bear to watch both of the boys go away on the same day."

One of the hardest things to hear is the sound of a mother weeping in the gallery.

Legal aid lawyers are important links in the chain of justice. I know this to be true because I see what happens to people who may not have access to someone like me because they have just a bit too much income to qualify for legal aid, but not enough income to hire a lawyer. So they represent themselves, which is not a wise way to proceed to a trial. Sometimes they might plead guilty or be found guilty because they don't understand the system. Everyone needs a competent lawyer.

If the Canadian criminal justice system didn't have legal aid lawyers, it would be a travesty. Not everybody is a law-abiding member of the community, but everybody is entitled to fairness. Every single one of us.

*When I first talked with Luann Jones, she made an instant impression. She was wearing a tie and a three-piece suit, her regular outfit for work. She is smart, brave, funny, confident, and a person of faith, which she thanks her maker for every day. She talked to me in glowing terms about the first responders she's encountered, and especially those she met during the pandemic. But then she paused and said with a smile, "I'm a last responder." And that she is. She's a funeral director.*

# THE FUNERAL DIRECTOR

## Luann Jones

I was standing in the embalming room at my funeral home in Scarborough, Ontario. I was alone, at least among the living. I had some music playing through the speakers as I prepared an elderly gentleman for burial. I had just finished washing his body with water and topical disinfectant, and was turning to arrange the embalming materials on a table when suddenly I felt a hand brushing my bum. No matter how long I'd been doing this work, I couldn't help but think, "Oh my God, is he still alive?"

He wasn't, of course. What had happened was I'd crossed his arms on his still damp and somewhat soapy chest, but they'd slid off, and one of his hands ran alongside my butt when I turned. As I gently brought his arms back to his chest, I looked at the body and said, "You just had to get one last feel, eh?"

When I was growing up, people used to ask me, "Luann, what do you want to be when you finish school?" And I'd reply that my dream job was to be a flight attendant. But I'm short, too short, I was told, to make the cut as a flight attendant. Then, when I was at high school, the guidance counsellor gave us tests to determine our strengths and potential career paths based on those strengths. Apparently, my answers showed I cared about others, stood by those in need, and enjoyed examining bugs and dissecting animals in science class. My results came back with a clear indication of what I might be good at—funeral director. I was shocked. There was no way I wanted to be a funeral director. I was so upset, I grabbed the test and did it again, but this time, I changed my answers, and it came back: hairdresser/cosmetologist.

During high school, I got pregnant twice, and by the time I was in my late teens, I was a single mother, but I didn't give up. I cared for my two beautiful boys, Jordan and Aaron, and I kept studying hard. My marks remained very good, and when I finally graduated at nineteen, I applied for the nursing program at Humber College in Toronto, which included taking more vocation tests.

I still remember the day the response to my application came in the mail. I got home that evening, opened the door while holding my son, and began tearing open the envelope.

I started screaming and jumping up and down. On my hip, Jordan said, "What happened, Mummy? What happened?"

"I'm accepted!" I shouted.

I looked at the letter again. Not only was I accepted, the school had been so impressed with my passion and care, they recommended I think about a job as—you guessed it—a funeral director. Did I really want to go into the business of the dead? I went to the Ontario Colleges website to find out more. Right up front, they warned that funeral directing is not for everyone. They also explained that there are many different aspects of the job, from the scientific (handling bodies) to the compassionate (understanding the grieving process), and upon graduation, students could fill any of these roles or a combination. And Humber had one of the top funeral director courses in Canada.

I decided to go for it. Why not? No harm in trying. After all, they wanted me.

It was during one of my first observation classes that I saw my first deceased person. She was a little old lady, about ninety years old. And when I looked at her, she just seemed to be in a deep, peaceful sleep. She looked beautiful. I knew then that there was dignity to be found in death, and my job would be to help give that to people.

I also learned that death is not always pleasant. You have to have the stomach for it. Literally. Early in that first semester, we came to class and stood in a room where there were about ten corpses. These were people who had donated their bodies to science. Now, corpses can have a bit of an odour; a trick of the trade is to line the inside base of your nostrils with Vicks VapoRub to avoid the unpleasant smell. But this early in our program, none of us knew that, and many in the class started to rock back and forth on their heels. Then side to side. Then a few passed out. Luckily, I stood firm. But that day was meant to be a test of who had what it took to be a funeral director. Believe it or not, there are hundreds of applicants each year for funeral director programs, and by the time graduation rolls around, less than a hundred receive degrees. I was one of them.

My family is from Guyana, and while most of my life has been in Canada, I'm strongly influenced by my family's connections with the Guyanese community. When I first began working in the funeral business, our friends—strongly influenced by generations of Guyanese ghost stories, or jumby stories as they call them—couldn't believe my choice of a profession. "Aren't you worried about the jumbies in a funeral home?" they'd ask. I'd just laugh. As a child, I used to love scary stories. In fact, I'd turn the lights off and watch scary TV shows on my own, and instead of shaking in my boots, I'd laugh. So when I'm asked about "jumbies," my comeback is always the same: "It's the living you should be afraid of, not the dead."

I love my work. I started in one of the lower-level jobs and worked my way up. I now own an independent funeral home, and others work for me. It's an essential job. In Canada, there are an average of 779 deaths a day and only 1,200 funeral homes, some national or internationally owned, others independent like me. Which is why it's important that we care about the well-being of the families that come to us. We have a multi-racial customer base. Death has no colour restrictions. Of course, the Guyanese community feels at home with me, but so does the Jamaican community. We also serve Filipino families, Italian families, Caribbean families, Chinese families, Indian families, and every religion and every culture here in Canada.

I'm passionate about making sure anyone who comes to our home is treated like they are the only one in that moment. Whether they are

*This photo was taken in 2019 on an emotional day for all of us at the Global Kingdom Ministry in Scarborough. It was the hugely attended funeral for one of the Toronto area's leading Black cultural figures, Fitzroy Gordon, often known as Mr. G 98.7 because he launched Canada's only Black and Caribbean radio station, 98.7FM.*

there for a burial, a cremation, or a memorial service, I want them to believe that me and my staff are there for them and no one else. After all, their lives have just been crushed. It may have come suddenly, or it may have been months or even years in the making. I've met with many families, and if there is a constant in their stories, it's that nothing prepares us for that final moment. It's at that time that we need a funeral director, but more, we need a friend. I try to be both.

While most of our clients have lost a loved one from natural causes, there are also those who arrive with a far different story. Burn victims, those who have died in car crashes, those murdered by gun violence. The stories are horrific, and the bodies show the horror. But the families will often look at me through their grief and still ask if an open casket is possible. I don't say no; I say I will do the best I can. It's in those moments that I remember the ninety-year-old from my first days at Humber. No matter the circumstance, I try to ensure everyone we prepare for their final moments has that same peaceful appearance. It gives me great pride to do the makeup and restoration, to help a family in a difficult circumstance see their loved one as they once were.

I've seen a lot, but the hardest ones are those who arrive at our home unclaimed. No family, no loved one, not a single person willing to stand at a service for the final goodbye. When I look down at these bodies as I ready them for burial, I remember that they began life as someone's child. They were a kid in grade school. They were a teenager. And as an adult, they must have lost their way, lost their friends, lost their journey. Yet here they are in my home, ready to depart this life. And I do my best to send them on their way with the best of care that their final days may not have seen. It's the least I can do.

I thank the Lord every day for blessing me with faith. For giving me the strength and resilience to tolerate and process what I see, whatever that is—good, bad, ugly. I remember one night I was working late. It was about two in the morning. I was literally putting somebody back together who had been terribly mangled in a motorcycle accident. I stood back and I said to myself, "Lord, who in their right mind would enjoy doing something like this?" And then I heard a voice saying, "Not only do you put people back together again, you bring broken families back together again."

That was how I knew that this was my ministry. Because people come into my funeral home, and they confide in me and find comfort in speaking with me. I use my skills, my life abilities, to shepherd them through their journey. They rely on me to get them through the grief, and as the last responder, I embrace that need.

*I've always had a thing about heights. No problem in a plane for some reason, but don't get me close to a window in a high-rise building. I can't look down or I get that funny tingling in my arms, legs, and stomach. I'm not alone. Among many others, I know a former prime minister who gets that feeling in an elevator, especially those windowed elevators, like the ones in the CN Tower in Toronto. So I wanted to know just how do those window washers who scale down skyscrapers do it, and why is it one of those jobs that actually makes Canada work? According to Noah Nava in Edmonton, it sure is.*

# THE WINDOW WASHER
## Noah Nava

There are thousands of tall buildings in Canada. Some of them are skyscrapers which, by definition, means they are at least 150 metres in height. Some of them are condos or apartments, some are office buildings. Whatever the case, they are the home or the workplace for literally millions of Canadians, all of whom I'm sure would like to see out their windows as they watch the grime of pollution build up and block their view. It's only natural that they want to work in a clean environment, and that's why they wipe their desks every day.

But the windows? They draw the line at hanging off the side of a building to do that. In our big cities, it doesn't take long for windows to get glazed with dirt, which means most of those big buildings need a cleaning at least twice a year. That leaves people like me getting out our squeegees and heading where most would never go to wipe the glass clean, no matter whether they're on the sixth floor or the sixty-sixth floor.

There are several ways to clean high-rise windows, but there are two main ones. You can work off a motorized platform that lowers floor by floor at your command, usually with at least one other worker on board cleaning the panes alongside you. Or you can operate like I do, cradled in a harness and sitting in a kind of bosun's chair or what we call a podium.

I have eight hundred feet of rope with me. It's *my* rope, which I'm responsible for storing and preparing, just like a paratrooper does with his or her parachute. Eight hundred feet of rope is heavy, often more than a hundred pounds. After I go over the edge at the top of the building, I control things as I go down. There are others working alongside me on their own lines, controlling their own rate of descent. And because I don't have a platform to hang the things I need with me, it means I have to carry them. Like a pail of water, enough to do all the windows I am responsible for all the way down, which could be as little as a hundred feet or often as much as eight hundred feet.

How did I find myself hanging over the side of a skyscraper? Well, I didn't just wake up one day and say, "Hey, I want to be a high-rise window washer!" then head out, grab a rope, and drop over the side. Nope. I was simply looking for a challenge.

I was born and raised in Red Deer, Alberta, and went to Red Deer College. Like a lot of my friends, after school, I headed north to work in the oil fields near Fort McMurray. I was a labourer working with concrete, which was hard work, cold work. I spent a lot of time wondering if there was something more challenging and more interesting to do than mixing concrete. I started focusing on the fellows going up the big rigs and towers with ropes. I was intrigued, which was ironic because when I was a child, I used to get a bit freaked out about heights. I decided I wanted to fight that fear, and I did.

I enrolled in a rigorous training program, which I passed, and I became a licensed rope access technician approved by the Alberta government. And that is the proper terminology to describe what I do. I'm not a window washer, I'm not a skyscraper climber, I'm a rope access technician, or RAT, in Edmonton. And what I learned was that to be good at this job, you have to be patient and focused—and always on guard for what could go wrong.

Like the weather. Weather can be our greatest enemy. Every morning, we do a weather check. If it's raining or snowing, we're not scaling the building. Edmonton winters are Edmonton winters, and that means it's often too cold for the dangle, and Edmonton summers can sometimes just be too hot. I've been on a building on a beautiful, calm summer day when it was almost impossible to wash the glass. Why? It gets so hot, and the *glass* gets so hot, that one swish with the squeegee and the water evaporates before I can do the cleaning stroke. Seriously. The glass gets *that* hot.

But the most dangerous weather element is wind.

I still remember one morning in 2021 when we were scheduled to clean a thirty-seven-storey building. Our team checked the weather. All looked just fine in the forecast, and it stayed that way for the first few hours as half a dozen of us scaled the building and began to clean the windows. Then all of a sudden, the wind picked up, not much, but fifteen to twenty kilometres an hour is enough to cause real havoc, and it certainly did. Within seconds, we were swinging around, seemingly with no control. I was a rookie in those days and immediately looked at my buddies to see what they were doing. There was a lot of intense eye contact. The response by shouting or hand waving was blunt: get down. The water in my bucket sloshed as I whipped around the building. But I also remembered my training. I holstered my squeegee and pulled out the suction cups we all carry to stick and hold us to the glass. It took two agonizingly long minutes, but finally we were all safe. Hundreds of feet above the ground, but safe. Slowly we worked our way down, one suction cup at a time until we were on solid footing once more. It was a teaching moment. Maybe we had been a bit complacent about the danger, but we never would be again.

I have a motto I follow every day; one I try to instill in the new RATs who join our team. It's very simple: "Missing one step means you miss every step." Everything I do from the minute I arrive on site until I've completed my windows and touched the ground is one in a series of steps that ensure my safety, hundreds of steps, not just that first one over the edge.

That's why we make risk or danger pay. It's also why we work contract—by the day and by the season—because the weather does often get in the way. But nothing beats the challenge of dangling from the side of a building hundreds of metres in the air. To me, it's worth it, and I know I'm not alone in that. A lot of people assume that RATs are all young guys, but like all professions, times have changed, and ours is no different. While most of my colleagues in this business are young men in their twenties or early thirties, there are a few young women working the high-rise windows in Edmonton and even some older men in their sixties. We love the dangle.

In the days before we arrive at a new building, all the occupants are advised that their windows are going to be washed and to keep that in mind. Maybe close curtains or lower blinds. But people either don't read the advisories or they forget, or they don't care. Or they're exhibitionists! I've seen them all. Office towers are no problem. Most people are at their desks working, and when we drop by, literally, they're a bit surprised but smile and wave. Or we'll drop by the area where employees have a break or take an exercise class, and they laugh and wave. Some even offer, if there are balconies or open windows, to get us a coffee or a muffin.

Private residences can be a different story. Given the time of day we do our job, most are empty as we squeegee by. But there is always at least one unit a day where the resident is either oblivious to us, or for some reason, wants us to watch. I've seen it all, and I mean, *all*. From using the bathroom to walking around naked to, yes, sex. My friends always ask, "Why don't you just look away?" Easy to say but sometimes hard to do when I'm on a rope, *facing* the window, and focused on cleaning it. That's why I'm there. It's a little hard to look away no matter how much I might want to.

People often ask me, "Do you ever get nervous?"

I do. Every day that I'm working there is one moment when I feel the tingling that those heights, or even the thought of heights, gives some of us. For me it's the moment where I'm standing on the roof of

*Another day on the dangle in Edmonton.*

the building and I'm about to go over the edge where there's nothing but air for hundreds of feet straight down.

I've already checked everything many times over, from my rope being perfectly positioned, to my water bucket properly attached to my belt, to my squeegee in its place with no chance of it falling into space (I've never dropped anything, and believe me, you don't want that to happen for all the obvious reasons). While, at this moment, standing near the edge, I'm absolutely confident that everything is 100 percent safe, I'm still nervous. I throw that first leg over the edge. I pull on my rope and get the firm response I'm expecting, and then it's that time. Time to go. My other leg goes over the edge, and instantly I'm there, bum on the podium, hanging in space. Ready for another day. Ready for the grime, ready for the smiles, the waves, the coffees, the weird sights. Ready.

*When you walk down the grocery store aisle, what do you think
about? Do you consider where all those products started their journey
to the shelves—who grew them, who produced them, who packaged
them? Who made the decision about what the price would be? Who
trucked it to the loading dock at the back of the store? Or, finally, who
put it on the shelf so you could pick it up? There are a lot of people
who "touched" that product before you moved it into your cart.
People like Rechev Browne, a grocery store supervisor in Toronto.*

---

# THE GROCER
## Rechev Browne

It was a dark, cold night in April 2020 when I left the subway station
and began my walk home. I'm a big strong guy in my late twenties,
but I was scared. Why? It wasn't a sketchy area, and I wasn't afraid of
getting mugged. I was afraid of being stopped by the police.

That month, Canadians had been told to stay at home, to shelter in
place because of the pandemic. It wasn't a suggestion; it was an order.

The only reason we were allowed to be outside was if we were on the way to or from work—and that work had to be essential work. As a shift supervisor at a No Frills grocery store in the Etobicoke area of Toronto, I was an essential worker. But I'm Black. And walking alone along the street near midnight, masked and bundled up, had me worried. I carried my documentation in an inside pocket, and it declared, as required, that I was an essential worker and needed to be outside to get to and from work, and it was signed by my boss. There was only one problem. If I was stopped and asked for documentation, I would have to reach into my breast pocket to retrieve it. And that's what had me scared. When you are young and Black and walking alone at night with your face covered, you don't want to find yourself in that position. Those of us who fit that profile know all too well stories that start like that but don't end well.

But nothing happened. No one stopped me. I never had to show proof that I was essential. I walked to my home, hugged my mom, and relaxed. Tomorrow would be another day. Another essential day in a workplace every Canadian depends on—a place where they can find everything they need to sustain their daily life.

I was born on one of those gorgeous Caribbean islands Canadians flock to every winter. Saint Vincent is just west of Barbados, north of Grenada, and south of Saint Lucia. They all might feel the same to tourists—palm trees, long stretches of sand, calypso music, and spectacular blue-green waters. But being from there, I know they're all very distinctive, Saint Vincent included. It's my original home and always will be. I have family there and try to get back every few years to visit them. In Saint Vincent, we have an old saying, "Circumstances make you who you are."

But Canada has given me opportunity and the ability to earn a reasonable living—both things I just couldn't achieve in Saint Vincent. I finished high school here in Canada and went to college, looking for a degree in retail sales, and eventually landed a job that has given me the opportunity to serve the public in a way that, let's face it, they couldn't live without.

At first, I worked at some small mom-and-pop corner stores doing odd jobs, but when I heard that a new No Frills store was about to open in our area, my employer and my mom said to go for it, and I did. Fifteen years later, I'd worked my tail off to become a supervisor, which means I'm in charge in the store on evening shifts. (The manager runs the show on the morning shift.) It can be a challenge overseeing a whole store, but I love it.

My primary focus is to ensure the store shelves are always stocked, so I'm constantly walking the aisles to check product levels. Toilet paper has always been the number one item that we run out of, even before COVID. But it was crazy during those early days of the pandemic. We ran out of toilet paper all the time, and I would move stacks of new supplies every half an hour. It didn't even matter what the price was, people would pay anything for toilet paper. Even my partner at the time would say, "Bring home more toilet paper." And I would reply, "What? We have toilet paper in the car, in the house, in your parents' house. We don't need more."

More than once, the shelves would go empty, and people would demand, "Where is the toilet paper? Can't you bring more out?" When they moved from upset to angry, I would get tempted to say, "What do you want me to do? Go in the back lot, cut down a tree, and start making toilet paper?" But of course, the customer is always right, so I couldn't do that. Instead I would try a 101 course in supply economics.

The three other best sellers are chips, sugar, and salt. Every day, I move new supplies in, sometimes more than once a day, just to keep the shelves full. We sell so much that if the daily supply truck arrives without sugar on it, the next day the sugar shelf will be empty. Moving sugar and salt around the store is not easy. The skids contain dozens of bags, each weighing fifty kilos, and pushing those a few times a day makes me wish people would consume less sugar, for their health and for mine! Chips aren't healthy either, but I can push a skid of chips with one hand.

In the first days of the pandemic, there was a high mark for people who have jobs like mine. What I mean is: Everyone was so nice to us. Media attention was focused on us in a way it never had been. We were called "essential workers," those who went to work, in effect risking our own health, while others were ordered to stay inside, protected by the four walls of their homes. We were *heroes*. We'd never been seen that way before. Never. But now people were thanking us all the time. I could rarely go from one aisle to the next without someone saying, "Thank you, you're so helpful" or "Thank you. Have a nice day." Just that little bit of humanity meant so much to me. It was all it took to make me smile, and in those early pandemic days, I smiled a lot.

We used to sit in the back room on breaks and share a laugh about all the nice things people were saying to us, and about us. Don't get me wrong, we loved it, but we knew it couldn't last. "When will we return to normal?" we'd say, borrowing the phrase everyone else was using on the outside, but it meant something different to us, and would always get a good chuckle.

Normal came to us in 2022. But with a twist. This time we weren't seen as saviours by our customers, but as part of the problem. Inflation cut through our store and grocery stores like us. Prices went up *a lot*, and low- to middle-income earners—our primary customers—were hurting. We call it "shrinkage," but others might call it "shoplifting."

In the best of times, stealing is a minor issue. During inflationary times, it's far from minor. We saw shoplifting go up significantly, and some cases were heartbreaking. One day, I was called to the front of the store where a young mother was with her toddler, looking scared and upset. She'd been seen pocketing a package of mac and cheese. As the supervisor, this was now my problem.

"Ma'am," I said gently, "you know you can't do this."

"I know, but my son was crying for it, and I just can't afford it."

I felt for her. I listened and consoled her, but only to a point. I couldn't ignore what she'd done. I had a heart, though. I didn't call the police; instead, I wrote out a formal warning, banned her from the

*It's not easy keeping customers happy, but the pandemic proved they appreciated us more than we realized.*

store, and sent her on her way. Nothing about that experience made me feel good. Sadly, there would be more times just like it.

I care about what I do. I care about the people I work with and the people I serve. I try to do the right thing no matter the circumstance, and sometimes the circumstances can be pretty challenging. There are times, quite a few, sadly, when it's not easy being Black in a service role in Canada. It's not uncommon to be called "boy" by some customers. And yes, I've had the N-word thrown in my face. I don't cower. I make it clear those terms are not acceptable in our store, where, as it happens, I'm not the only person of colour on staff. It's moments like that when you want management to put aside their tired old refrain about the customer always being right. That just implies the fallacy that in times of dispute, the employee is always wrong.

These past few years have taught me a lot about life. Whenever there's catastrophe, whenever there's conflict, we band together. Kumbaya. But whenever it gets easy and there's no tension, we just go back to thinking of ourselves. You're over there. I'm over here. Whenever there's tragedy, we're all in this together. Community, right? And then we forget.

Most days I really enjoy my job. The responsibility. The dealing with customers, both the nice ones and the angry ones. And I enjoy the fact that my job matters to a lot of people. I'm putting food on the shelves so people can eat. I'm a critical part of the food chain, in many ways just as important as the farmer who started the chain. If I didn't exist, there would be no food on your table. Not to mention the toilet paper.

But it's like that old saying from Saint Vincent: "Circumstances make you who you are." I saw that with how we were seen during the pandemic. I saw that with some customers forced to steal during high inflation. And now I'm seeing it with me as I consider a different path to the future.

### Postscript

*Rechev resigned from his job just before this book was published. He's now in construction earning a better hourly wage and is a member of a construction trades union, something he was not able to achieve in the grocery business. He's still making the country work.*

*When most of us think about babies being delivered, we*
*probably see a doctor at work. After all, doctors were there*
*for about eighty-five percent of the almost 370,000 births*
*in Canada last year, according to Statistics Canada. What*
*about the other fifteen percent? Well, midwives help make the*
*system work and Debbie Vey's story explains how. Debbie is*
*just one of fifteen registered midwives in Saskatchewan.*

---

# THE MIDWIFE
## Debbie Vey

Midwives were part of life when I grew up in southern England in the 1970s. A woman who became pregnant routinely went to see a midwife, not a doctor. When I had my three children in the 1990s, they were all delivered with the help of midwives.

I originally trained as a nurse. Then when I had my stint in the maternity ward, I just fell in love with it. Birth is such a wonderful, private experience to be part of, and when I place a newborn on the mother's chest, it's an emotional moment that I can hardly describe in words. After I completed my nursing education, I went on to do my midwifery education, which took another eighteen months.

As a midwife, I helped women through their pregnancies and the birthing process and afterwards. If you've seen *Call the Midwife*, a TV show about a group of midwives in a poorer district of London in the 1950s and 1960s, that's a good reference point for what a midwife does. While I didn't get on my bicycle with my little bag like those midwives did, I did develop close relationships with the pregnant mothers and their newborns as shown in the program, and as a midwife, I was able to reach more vulnerable populations that might live far from the city centre or not have access to the medical system.

I was very happy as a midwife in England, where my husband and I and our three children lived on a farm. It was a sizeable farm by English standards, about a hundred acres. Of course, in Canada that's laughably small. Over time, we found it more and more difficult to make any money by farming, and we both had to have outside jobs to make ends meet. My husband worked in the petro-chemical business, and I worked part-time as a midwife. As a family, we decided to consider emigrating.

Our choices came down to Canada or Australia. Australia is certainly warmer, but they have a lot of poisonous things, like snakes and spiders. At the time, we both had family living in England, and we thought it would be easier to visit them if we lived in Canada. Before we made a final decision, we came to Saskatchewan and Manitoba to look around, and the kids loved the snow. We'd never seen snow so deep. I think people thought we were completely nuts because we were all playing in the snow. So, in 2006, we bought land north of Lipton, Saskatchewan, and went from a hundred acres to 4,000 acres. Over the years, we've had cows and sheep, and we've grown grain.

When we settled in Saskatchewan, I thought everyone would know all about midwives, but when I told people I was a midwife, I was often met with a blank stare. Almost no one knew what I was talking about. I learned that though there were some midwives working in Saskatchewan, there was no legislation making it a publicly funded profession like it was in England. In other words, women who wanted a midwife had to pay for it.

So when people asked me what I did, I started answering, "I'm a registered nurse."

"How fantastic!" they'd say. "We need nurses. Welcome."

I was planning to devote myself to farming, but one day, a neighbour up the road told me that All Nations' Healing Hospital in Fort Qu'Appelle was looking for nurses. I thought that might be a good way to make some extra money, so I popped into the hospital. As it turned out, the manager I met with had been a midwife earlier in her life, and I was hired to develop a new program in our First Nation communities. But my timing was very good because the idea of having registered midwives available to provide local care across the province was starting to gain traction, and two years later, in 2008, Saskatchewan adopted the Midwifery Act, which made midwifery a provincially recognized, self-regulating, and publicly funded profession. With the backing of Health Authorities, midwifery programs sprang up in Saskatoon, Regina, Swift Current, and Fort Qu'Appelle, to serve both urban and surrounding rural communities.

Until then, most pregnant women in our area had to see an obstetrician in Regina, driving an hour each way for every prenatal appointment, and to give birth there as well. For women in more rural areas, there was limited prenatal care (and it's still very difficult in Northern Saskatchewan). But now we had the opportunity to reach women closer to home, and those who would be considered high risk. Midwives were also encouraged to target a priority population—those that were very young, immigrants, and First Nation and Métis women. In Fort Qu'Appelle, we were also now able to offer birthing closer to home by opening our birthing centre.

After the Midwifery Act, we opened the Women's Health Centre in Fort Qu'Appelle where women get full midwifery care, which means we see them throughout the prenatal period, and then we're with them through their labour and birth (even if they choose to have their baby at the hospital in Regina, where we have privileges) and then we follow up with them postpartum for six to eight weeks. During that time, we develop a close relationship with our clients. (I never call them patients. That makes it sound as if they're sick, which they are not. Birthing is a normal, natural process.)

Some of the first clients I saw were Indigenous women. As I quickly learned, they already knew what midwifery was all about. They had traditionally relied on an older woman in the community to help deliver their babies, and now they were accessing the new programs, one of which was geared specifically to First Nation women.

Today, the Women's Health Centre is attached to the All Nations' Healing Hospital, a facility which provides cultural and traditional services in addition to twenty-four-hour health care, emergency care, and much more. We typically provide midwifery care to about six clients a month. And in 2014, we had our first birth at the birthing centre.

Part of what we do at the Women's Health Centre specifically is establish relationships with obstetricians or other care providers in Regina. We have good relationships with most doctors. There's the odd one who believes they're higher on the medical hierarchy, but they're the exception. Most obstetricians agree that for low-risk birthing, midwifery is totally appropriate. Fewer family doctors are delivering babies, so the case load for obstetricians is getting heavier, and most don't need the extra work. I recall an obstetrician at Regina General who had originally practiced in New Zealand, where midwives are also very common, and his attitude was, "Where are all the midwives? Why aren't they running the show? Why am I being called in to do a low-risk birth?"

When a woman seeks out midwifery care, she's usually done some research and understands we're all about putting the woman first, to give her the care that's appropriate for her circumstances. I always say to them, "It's your pregnancy, your body, your baby." A doctor might say to them, "Here's a prescription for iron. Go for this test. Then go for that ultrasound." Midwifery philosophy is to provide more informed choice and emotional support. We have thirty- to forty-five-minute appointments with our clients where we have time to discuss what we're recommending and why. But the final choice is the woman's. If she chooses to follow my advice, that's fine. If she chooses not to, we discuss the pros and cons of her choice.

If there's a reluctance to see a midwife, it usually comes from the partner or mother of the pregnant woman who is worried about what happens in an emergency. Some people think if you're going to a midwife, you're going to be delivering in the bush somewhere. They don't understand that we are a regulated profession, that we have education, that we can order blood work, ultrasound investigations, whatever is necessary, and are able to deal with emergencies. I encourage partners

*One of our mothers, Danielle Babcock, practices neonatal
resuscitation with instructor Melanie Keisg, who is
holding baby Asher, at the Women's Health Centre.*

and family to come in to the office at the Women's Health Centre
so we can also discuss with them what we can do. It's important to
reassure everyone involved that the woman and the baby will be well
cared for. A partner, a grandmother, whoever has doubts. In fact, one
mother actually asked to see my credentials. It's happened only once,
but I was happy to prove I was qualified and registered. If that gave her
a bit of reassurance, I didn't mind at all.

All midwives have training for emergencies. We have and can give
medication for postpartum hemorrhaging in the mother. Sometimes
the baby just doesn't breathe as quickly or as efficiently as it should,
and we can do resuscitation for newborns. In Fort Qu'Appelle, we also

introduced a program called "MOREOb" (managing obstetrical risks effectively), because yes, sometimes things don't go quite the way we've planned. We are attached to a hospital with a 24/7 emergency centre. On top of that, we can transfer someone by ambulance in about forty-five minutes to Regina General, where they have more resources. But most of the time we don't need any of that. We have had more than 130 babies come into the world at our birthing centre since we opened. All were delivered normally and healthy, with fewer than 5 percent needing extra assistance, and their mothers have done well too.

I can't emphasize enough that midwives are a good option for a low-risk pregnancy, but not for every pregnancy. I don't hesitate to tell a woman she should see an obstetrician. I've had women tell me, "I really want a natural birthing experience outside the hospital with a midwife." But if I see she's got quite a long list of complicating circumstances or she's had previous difficulties in pregnancy, the services of a midwife alone are not suitable. I don't turn her away, though. I tell her I can provide shared care, which is the out-of-the-box thinking so often necessary in a rural setting. This means I can look after her for some of the prenatal care, which is comforting because sometimes obstetricians can be in a bit of a rush, and if she has questions or needs clarification, I have time to discuss them during her appointment. The doctor will be there for the birth at Regina General Hospital, and then I can follow up postpartum.

As a midwife, I'm on call 24/7. Sometimes I can be up for twenty-four hours straight, dealing with a woman in pain. It's good pain, because as I tell the woman, it means the labour is progressing, but it's still pain. Nowadays, the partners and support people are in the room, not pacing the floor outside like they might have done in the past when birthing was considered a woman's thing. Some are gung-ho, fired up, asking questions, always wanting to know what's happening now and what's going to happen next. I tell them to just take their cues from me. If I'm relaxed and just waiting, maybe that's what they should be doing too.

Being a midwife can be physically and mentally draining. As I get older, I find I don't bounce back quite as quickly as I used to from those long hours. But midwifery is a vocation. It's not a job. This is what I wanted to do. The greatest secret that midwives have is that we actually don't deliver babies. It's the mums who deliver babies. The babies could be born most of the time without us being there. But we are there. And every single time, it is awe-inspiring. When I hear that baby cry, and I bring the baby to the mum's tummy, it's very emotional. I'm extremely grateful to be involved in what is a very private time for the woman and her partner. It's an experience I can't really put into words.

The mother usually thanks me for being there, and I say, "Thank you for letting me come on this journey with you, and for putting your trust in me."

And while Mum has done all the work, I refer to the babies I've helped into the world as "my babies." The benefit of living in Fort Qu'Appelle is that I get to see them grow up. When I see them at seven or eight years old, going to school, I remember them as babies and that moment when I first heard them cry.

*How the prison system and equally, the parole system, operates is a bit of a mystery to most of us. Just what happens inside those walls? And how inmates can claim their rehabilitated behaviour should allow them a new chance on the outside is often a controversial discussion. Patrick O'Brien is a full-time member of the national Parole Board, one of fewer than sixty people who are full-time parole officers across Canada. He's worked throughout the country, and is now based in Moncton, New Brunswick, as part of the Board's Atlantic Regional office.*

◆

# THE PAROLE BOARD MEMBER
## Patrick O'Brien

As a Parole Board member, I often hear the allegation that Canada is soft on crime, and the Parole Board of Canada is a big part of that because it opens prison doors for hardened criminals to get back on our streets.

I was once at a conference in the States to deliver a presentation on how we assess whether it's appropriate or not to release an offender on parole. When I was finished, there was a guy at the back of the room who piped up. "That's all kind of interesting stuff you talked about," he said. "But I haven't heard you say, 'He ain't done enough time.' "

Right to the point. And though it was an American expressing that view, it's an argument with legs in Canada too. Let me tell you what I said then, and what I say today.

I stay in my lane. If the government ever changes the law as it applies to parole, or as it applies to sentencing, that's fine. But it's not my job to argue with the law. It's my job to work within the framework that our justice system has established. I'm part of what I believe is a fair, transparent, and accountable process.

I get my schedule about three weeks in advance, and I typically have one day of preparation, then a day of hearings, then repeat. So if I have three hearings on a Tuesday, I'll spend Monday electronically pulling up all the information that's been generated on the offenders I'll be seeing. Their criminal records, trial records, parole reports, prison behaviour. It's very thorough.

Hearings take place either in person at the penitentiary or remotely via videoconference. The majority of cases are heard by two board members, and we review the files independently of each other. I've been at this for more than fourteen years now—I'm in my third five-year appointment—so I'm probably one of the most experienced Parole Board members in Canada, which means I often lead the hearing. I'll ask the bulk of the questions, but my colleague is free to ask questions and seek clarification on any points at any time.

I start by introducing ourselves, and then I call on a hearing officer to go over a lot of procedural safeguards. That person explains how

*At my desk reviewing documents in advance of a day of hearings.*

the hearing will unfold and makes sure the offender understands their rights and responsibilities.

Then I turn to the parole officer (who works for the Correctional Service of Canada, not the Parole Board) and ask for their recommendation, and the rationale for their recommendation. They explain why they think this offender is a good candidate for either day parole or full parole. Or why they don't think he's a good candidate. Next, I ask the offender directly if what they heard was an accurate overview of their case and if they are ready for us to ask them questions.

All our questions follow what we call a structured decision-making framework. There's quite a science to risk assessment. Not a perfect science, but strong science—the framework has a high success rate.

We know the factors that speak to a higher likelihood of reoffending versus those factors that tend to inhibit reoffending, and we ask a lot of behavioural-based questions to see on which side of the ledger the answers fall.

If I know that the offender has had a lot of unstable relationships and starts using drugs or goes back to liquor, or connects with the old gang of fellow criminals when relationships end, I'd put that scenario to him. I'd ask, "What if you're on parole and your girlfriend decides to break up with you. How are you going to respond to that?"

Then I'd put another scenario to him. "You've been inside for a number of months, and now you're out. You've been a hard drinker for a long time, and though you say you're ready to quit, you're still young, and it's Friday night, and the music's playing as you walk by all the bars. What are you going to do?"

If he answers, "I'll call my sponsor," that's not enough. I'd press him to tell me what skills he has to make sure he doesn't put himself in that high-risk situation to begin with. Or tell me the practical, realistic things he's going to do to get out of that situation. I know how he's handled these things in the past. What I need to hear from him is how he would handle them now.

I've read everything about the person in front of me. The past is a static factor. That's not going to change. What I'm looking for are all the aspects of his personality and his lifestyle and his circumstances that might reveal to me that he now has new skills and knowledge so that he can insulate himself against what he has not been able to handle before. The trauma that so many people in the criminal justice system have experienced in terms of being abused or neglected is real and important to consider, especially for Indigenous and racialized offenders, which is why we provide Elder- and culturally-assisted hearings to meet their specific needs. But I also want to explore and talk about how they have improved themselves so the past doesn't result in bad outcomes forever.

The hearing room is not a courtroom. It's not an adversarial process. My job is to review all the relevant information I have before me and apply it to the risk framework to make an informed decision. The offender is entitled to an assistant: a person of their choice. It could be a lawyer, but it could also be his mother. The assistant doesn't have any special status. Their role is to help the offender. They might lean over and say, "You should expand on that point. They want to hear you talk about that." And at the end of the hearing, the assistant has the right to speak on behalf of the offender. But there's no right of cross-examination.

As an independent administrative tribunal, we don't retry the case that put the offender in prison. We accept the findings of the court. I once had a guy in front of me who'd been in prison for thirty-one years. Right off the bat, he said, "You know I didn't do it." All I could tell him was that he was free to fight his conviction, but I noted that he'd been rejected at appeal twice, and telling me he was innocent was not going to get him anywhere. That was a guy who thought there was nothing in his character that needed to change, and who wasn't going to take any programs in prison to improve himself because he thought taking programs was an admission of guilt.

I look for change in an offender. There was none in his case.

Then there are the cases that trigger most people's sense of judgment—child molestation and various sexual offenses. It's not my job to judge the morality of the offender. The court, in its wisdom, has made a sentencing decision, and now I have to make a decision on what is a safe and manageable release. The science will tell you that many of these offenders are quite manageable. Even if I can't envision any circumstances under which this person could ever be released, I can't close my mind. As repugnant as some things are—and I can recall doing four or five sex offender cases in a day that really wore me down—I can't dismiss the possibility of change.

It's also possible for victims of crime to be at a hearing. Survivors and victims of crime may have produced a victim impact statement at trial, which I will have read, but they also have the right to speak at the hearing about what the possible parole of the offender means to them. Typically, the victims who participate in a hearing have experienced a violent crime. The parole decision in a case involving significant violence or death, or sexual offending, is already very difficult. Adding this extra human element can be quite powerful. Everything suddenly becomes vivid. What the offender did had real consequences to real people, and it adds another dimension to what I read in the files. When a human being puts a face to the family and to the offense, it keeps me grounded. The voice of the victim is not a veto, but it's an important voice.

Victims almost always conduct themselves with incredible composure and are respectful of the process. I've seen victims shuffle out of the room pretty darn quick because they feel disgusted just seeing the offender, but outbursts are rare. I do recall a hearing that involved a woman in prison for killing a friend. The victim's father was in attendance. After some line of questioning, he jumped up and shouted something. The parole officer thought the father was going to come at the offender, so he jumped up too. I addressed the father, "Sir, I would really like you to stay in this room. It's important for us that you be here and be part of this hearing. So please just sit down." He did. We finished the hearing, and we authorized the offender's release.

As I left the penitentiary, the father approached me. I didn't know quite what to expect and tensed up a bit. But he extended his hand to shake mine, and he said, "Thank you for this." He was grateful for our Parole Board staff who had supported him through the ordeal, and he told me the hearing had been thorough and fair. I thought to myself, "Wow, I didn't see that coming."

Every decision made by a Parole Board hearing must be unanimous. After we've heard all there is to hear, I adjourn the hearing while I discuss the decision with my colleague. It's not necessarily a long conversation. We could agree that the hearing confirmed what the file said—that the offender is not ready for release. Or it could be the opposite of that. I've had only five or six cases that resulted in a split decision and required a new hearing with new Board members hearing the case. The majority of the time, we agree, which speaks volumes about the effectiveness of the training we've had in applying the risk framework.

It's very common for offenders who are granted parole to be sent to a halfway house for six months, and around 99 percent of those people succeed. Those who don't make it are usually returned to prison for technical violations of the conditions of their release—they have lapsed back into drugs or alcohol, for example, as opposed to committing a new crime.

Have I made mistakes? Have I released somebody who then failed to honour the terms and conditions of the release? Yes. But the failure of an offender is not going to make me lose faith in the framework that got me to the decision I made. In Canada, the vast majority of sentences have a fixed term. So offenders will come out from behind bars one day. Those who are supervised on parole before their eventual release commit fewer offenses of a less-serious nature than those who just go out the door with a handshake, five bucks, and a bus ticket. Sending someone to a halfway house means they have a place to live, they are supervised, and they are held accountable.

If there's one thing Canadians can be assured of, it's that the system is not weak, and it's not haphazard. By the time a person's case is presented to us, they've been in prison for a period of time, during which a serious effort has been made to identify all the risk factors of the offender: psychological assessments, follow-up programs, some of which take months to complete. When those programs are over, there's an independent assessment of how well, or poorly, the offender did. Parole officers also look to see if offenders have strengthened family contacts, and if they have a healthy living routine. It's with that information that they're presenting the cases and recommending release or saying they think the offender isn't ready. Only then is it time for me, independently, to make the final decision.

Nothing is more important in my work than public safety. That's our paramount consideration. I believe, and our system believes, that a person is capable of change under certain terms and conditions. I'm promoting public safety by making an informed decision about when a person is ready to serve part of their sentence in the community rather than in a prison.

Being a Parole Board member is not a career, it's an opportunity to serve. It's an extraordinary responsibility to render judgments on people's liberty that affects not only them, but also the victims of crime, and the community as a whole. It's a responsibility I never take lightly.

*Everyone knows Canadarm and its younger sibling, Canadarm2.*
*But do you know who operates it during the delicate missions*
*that happen high above us in space? Clue number one—the*
*operator isn't in space. She or he is on the ground, at a high-tech*
*mission control centre. Danielle Cormier is one of those operators,*
*based at the Canadian Space Agency in Longueuil, Quebec.*

◆

# THE SPACE OPERATOR
## Danielle Cormier

On most nights, if you look up into the sky, you can see the International Space Station fly by as it orbits the Earth every ninety minutes. After the moon, it's the brightest object in the night sky. It's 400 kilometres above us, weighs about 420,000 kilograms, and moves at a speed of more than eight kilometres a second. Since November 2000, people have continuously lived on board the ISS, conducting scientific research. And I helped build it.

Space has been part of my life since I was five years old. I grew up in Amos, Quebec, looking at the stars and dreaming of outer space. One of the first books I got was an astronomy book, and I told my mother then and there that I wanted to become an astronomer. In high school, I learned about Space Camp at the U.S. Space & Rocket Center in Huntsville, Alabama, and I asked my mom to take me. This was in the 1980s, when the U.S. Space Shuttle program began regular missions into outer space with a goal of building a permanently crewed Earth-orbiting station. In Canada, the government had announced its intention to create the Canadian Space Agency, which it did in 1989. To her credit, my mom looked into Space Camp and decided she wasn't just going to take me, she was going to take a group. She did that for seven years, and though I only went twice, it solidified my desire to pursue a career in space—not as an astronomer, but as an engineer. I wanted to be a part of creating the mechanics that would allow us to physically explore space and learn more about the universe we're part of.

So, after studying mechanical engineering at Polytechnique Montréal, I got a co-op student placement at the Canadian Space Agency. Four months in, they offered me a job. That's how I came to help build the International Space Station.

But first I went to NASA in Houston to train as a flight controller. Flight controllers are the people sitting at the computer consoles in Mission Control, aiding space missions in real time. While it's the most junior position, it takes three years of training to become certified, and a lot of that time is spent testing our responses when things go wrong or an anomaly pops up. We sat in simulation after simulation where trainers threw everything they could think of at us, and we had to make the right decisions and communicate with other members of the team to fix problems. It's intense—we were put through some catastrophic scenarios. We hope we never see those situations in real life, but if we did, we know how to respond.

As I was completing my certification, the creation of the International Space Station was already underway. Canada was one of fifteen countries that partnered to build and maintain the ISS, and what we provided were robotic systems, notably Canadarm2, a robotic arm completed in 1981 to bring material (payloads) into space and deploy and maneuver them. The station itself wasn't launched as a complete structure. It was assembled piece by piece, the first of which was launched into space in 1998.

For the next two years, more pieces were added to create the preliminary stages of the station. That's where I came in. While the original Canadarm, which was part of the Space Shuttle, was helping put the Space Station together, the Canadian Space Agency was already at work on a second robotic arm, and I was part of the team testing it.

At seventeen metres long and almost 1,500 kilograms, Canadarm2 is a larger, more advanced version of the original Canadarm. It has greater range of motion (it can travel the length of the ISS), degree of freedom (it's very similar to a human arm), joint rotation, and operating speed. While the original Canadarm returned to Earth after every shuttle mission, Canadarm2 is designed to remain permanently in space on board the ISS. It also boasts four-colour cameras, can be repaired in space, and can be operated from either space or the ground. Originally, we thought the astronauts in the Space Station were going to fly it around. But astronauts don't have time to do that. They're there to do science. So we started a series of software modifications that increased our ground control.

In 2001, Canadarm2 was completed and ready to launch. I was one of three team members who would support the mission. On April 19, we launched Canadarm2 into space onboard Space Shuttle *Endeavour*, which was also carrying the original Canadarm and Canadian astronaut Chris Hadfield, who would use the Canadarm to attach Canadarm2 to the ISS.

Three days later, I was in the control centre for the milestone moment when Chris, aboard the Canadarm, deployed its younger sibling.

Once the arm was assembled and attached to the station, congratulations rang out, but then we ran into trouble. The ISS main computer failed. We had a backup, but that also failed. Our third backup failed. This wasn't a simulation. This was real life.

At first, we were worried that the complexity of Canadarm2 was causing the problem. That turned out not to be the case—it was the ISS computers themselves that were glitching—but we still had to fix the problem. New hard drives were flown to the station. Until they arrived, we had to use the main computers a little differently, and when the new hard drives were installed, we all breathed a sigh of relief.

On April 28, Canadarm2 handed its launch cradle back to its older sibling in what became known as the "handshake in space." And with that, a new phase of construction began, and I was there for it all, including the 2008 launch of Dextre, an extension of Canadarm2 with smaller arms that can do more detailed work, like changing out small electronics. Dextre is the most sophisticated space robot ever built; it can actually perform more complex movements than a human arm, which means astronauts don't have to do as many risky spacewalks to make repairs because we can do them from Earth. The astronauts can spend more time on their scientific work.

I'm ROBO (Robotics Operations Officer) and I lead one of the three-person teams that send all the commands to make those robots move the way we need them to move. I'm in the mission control centre that you've probably seen on TV or in movies. In the past, that room was full of white men in white shirts. Now it's much more diverse. It's not all men. It's not all white. And thankfully, nobody smokes in the control centre anymore.

From my position, I'm in communication with the heads of all the disciplines like life support, navigation, and propulsion. That means I need more soft skills than in most engineering work. I've got to be able to communicate with dozens of different people in stressful situations. Basically, every time I'm going to maneuver Canadarm2 or Dextre, I have to ask everyone else, "Can I please do this? Is everything checked?"

I sit in front of a huge console with very large monitors that display telemetry from the Space Station and our robotics. There are probably

*At my post at the Canadian Space Agency in Longueuil, Quebec.*

10,000 pieces of data flowing, but not all of them are relevant at every moment. I can use the information to know the position of each of the joints of Canadarm2 and its motors.

We also have several cameras on the robotic systems, and we have cameras on the outside of the Space Station, so that if we're close to something, we can always see the clearance, and we can align properly if we're going to grab something. There are always a few seconds of lag between the time I send a command to space, the robotics respond, and the telemetry or imagery come back, but that's something I am used to.

By 2011, the ISS was complete. Today, it's a fully functioning science laboratory focused on researching future space exploration. But much of the research has improved life on Earth as well, from better weather predictions to advanced technology (products such as air purifiers, cellphone cameras, cordless vacuum cleaners, to name a few developed as spinoffs from space technologies).

As for Canadarm2 and Dextre, today they are operated from our controller booths on Earth, 98 percent and 100 percent of the time, respectively. Even though the ISS is finished, there is still much for Canadarm2 and Dextre to do. Cargo vehicles arrive regularly to replenish the ISS with supplies, or new experiments, or even spare parts. Some of those vehicles can dock directly on the station, but some just fly underneath, and we capture them with Canadarm2. We can unload the vehicle and put things where they belong. And when a part fails on the station, such as an electronics box, we often use our robotics to fix it.

We're quite busy. We use Canadarm2 two or three times a week, but it takes several days to plan each operation because we have to map every little motion and check with multiple people to make sure we're doing everything safely. Some operations are fairly simple, but there are always surprises. Recently, I worked on changing out one of the cameras on Canadarm2, which we'd never changed before. Because it was a new operation, we had to figure it out step by step, coordinating with everyone at Mission Control.

It's very difficult to do anything in less than six hours. But sometimes it takes eighteen hours or even twenty-four hours. We rotate our teams to handle those operations because no one can be anything but 100 percent alert. We are always watching for anomalies. A system could fail. A bug in the software could appear suddenly. Or there could be a problem elsewhere on the station that causes the arm to lose power in the middle of a move. It's my job to handle those situations. That's why they trained me so thoroughly—to be ready to deal with anything.

After twenty years of operating our robotics, we've become good at it, but nothing is routine. The truth is, we all mess up occasionally. When that happens, I try to absorb the lessons learned and work out anything I could have done differently, so the next time it's less likely I'll mess up again. The Space Station is the most expensive thing ever built. It cost about $200 billion CAD. We don't have any fail-safe system that will shut down Canadarm2 if it's about to collide with another part of the station. All we have are thorough procedures and trajectories that are checked by multiple people, to ensure we never have a disaster. Even still, there's always the question in the back of my mind: "Did I miss something?"

But I wouldn't have it any other way. I still remember dreaming of space when I was a little girl. Now, I get to tell people I'm a mission controller with the Canadian Space Agency, that I operate robots in space. They usually ask me if I want to go into space myself. My answer is "Not anymore." As a flight controller, I am paid to be paranoid. I am paid to know all the ways that systems can fail. I know too much. So, it's a little difficult to say, "Okay, I'd be happy to sit on top of the rocket." I've also been around when the toilet stops working on the Space Station. I want no part of that.

I'm quite happy sitting at my booth on Earth, while hundreds of kilometres above me, the International Space Station orbits.

*David Mitchell is a program manager at Insite, the first supervised safe injection site in North America. Insite is in a three-story building at Hastings and Main, the heart of Vancouver's Downtown Eastside. That neighbourhood is at the epicentre of Canada's drug overdose crisis, which has killed more than 30,000 people from 2016 through 2021.*

---◆---

# THE INSITE MANAGER
## David Mitchell

Nothing prepares you for the first overdose you see.

I remember the first time I saw an overdose at Insite. My heart raced, then my adrenaline kicked in. Somebody's life was on the line, and I was responsible for it. At the centre, I'm never alone—there's always at least one person with me—but things move very fast.

When an overdose happens, someone calls out, "crash kit" or "overdose." Then we try to stimulate the person, try to get a pain response out of them by tapping on the trapezius muscle on the upper back and neck. Sometimes that will snap a person out of what we call "a heavy nod," not a severe overdose.

But if someone's hypoxic, if they're turning blue, they're really overdosing. For those who have never seen an overdose, they may think it's like cardiac arrest and expect us to do chest compressions. But it's not like that. An overdose causes respiratory suppression. The most important thing we have to do is get the person air. So, we immediately bring them down to the floor and administer oxygen. We start bag-valve masking, where we secure a mask that's attached to a bag over the face and push air into the person's lungs by squeezing the bag, and we set up an oxygen monitor so we can see if the person's oxygen level improves.

We also inject naloxone, which reverses the effects of opioids in the body, and ideally it should take effect in about two minutes. If it doesn't, we inject a second dose.

When I started at Insite in 2016, we had six or seven overdoses, not every day, but every shift, and it wasn't unusual to handle two at the same time. At the end of each shift, I needed real decompression time and to find ways to reset before the next day. It was a very intense time to learn the job. Now, we see overdoses probably once or twice a shift, but it never gets routine.

We know drug use exists, and opioids in particular take thousands of lives every year. Our current health care system and emergency services are not equipped to properly respond to everyone suffering from addiction, especially those from marginalized communities. That's where Insite comes in—we are a harm-reduction program that provides a clean and safe environment for users to consume illicit drugs without the risk of spreading infectious diseases, and if something goes wrong, we're there on site to help. Our aim is to meet people where they're at and work with them to help meet their goals, however those look, and if they're interested, connect them to additional support such as detox and recovery treatment, and even housing needs.

When people find out what I do for a living, the reaction is usually positive. Most of Vancouver sees Insite as an essential public health service. Not everyone, though. Some ask, "How can you do that? You're just enabling people." I believe that no one would say that if they had direct experience with people who've been drug users, if they knew someone personally in their lives who used drugs. I'm someone who has had that experience.

My youngest brother was a drug user. He was very open about his struggles with substances and had been using on and off since his twenties. During a particularly tough spot in his life, he overdosed one night in a back alley in Vancouver's Downtown Eastside. That overdose was reversed by both community members and staff at Insite. He's the reason I got into this work.

Like many of my colleagues, I had zero background in the field. No education that had anything to do with drugs or harm reduction. I've learned everything through hands-on experience. A few people come here who have trained in addiction services, perhaps in counselling services or psychology. But that doesn't always mean they're able to handle this job.

Despite what some may think, this is a people job. We're not here just to rush in with the naloxone and oxygen when something goes wrong. The people we serve are starving for connection. I maintain professional boundaries, but I also need to make them feel as though they're part of something. This is their site. It was started at a grassroots level by drug users for drug users. Part of what we all do is saving lives, but I place more focus on ensuring the site is useful for the folks who access it. Feedback from the community is essential.

For the most part, those folks are the people who live in the Eastside, either on the street or in some kind of supported housing. Occasionally, someone from the nine-to-five crowd will show up. It's infrequent, but it does happen. When I went to my initial training, one of the first experiences I had was with a young guy in a university sweatshirt in his early twenties. He looked like anyone's brother or son. Our primary demographic is mostly males in their twenties to mid-forties, and Indigenous people are overrepresented.

We have our regular participants—that's how we refer to the people who come in because they're participating in a harm-reduction program—but we see fresh faces all the time. Some who have been using alone and realize it's unsafe. Others who have overdosed once or twice, or maybe they've had a friend overdose, and they think to themselves, "I'm at this particular state in my life, but I don't want to die." So they come in. We try to have a very welcoming environment where people can just come in, have a clean place to use, knowing there's staff willing to provide care if you need it.

That's one of the reasons we don't have security. There's also a power dynamic that exists, which many people don't realize. For example, I've seen the participants who are 6' 8" and covered in tattoos walk in the door, but when he sits down at a booth, I'm in the power position. And I have to be cognizant of not abusing that by making anyone feel lesser. So no security guards. When trouble does pop up, we rely on many deescalation strategies. Very often it's our participants who take ownership of the solution, especially those who have been coming to us for a long time. "Sit down, man," they'll say. "Don't ruin this." They know what it took to get our place up and running, and they want to keep it that way.

We operate as an almost entirely anonymous service. When a new participant arrives, there's a brief signup where we have a conversation in which they can give us as much or as little information as they want to. A lot of our participants have had negative experiences with more regimented intakes in medical settings, so it's important that we just talk and get to know them a little better—not read a list of questions.

We run over some of the basic guidelines of our site. Mostly golden rule stuff—be respectful to other participants and the staff. We let them choose a handle or code name to use when they come in again. Some choose a simple name like their initials and the last two digits of their year of birth, so something like RT99. Some choose more colourful names. My favourite was, "Only God Can Jug Me," which is a reference to the practice of injecting into the jugular vein.

After that, we enter them into our computer database, which is secured and confidential, then they take a seat in our waiting room until a staff person calls their handle. Once they disclose what drugs they're going to be using, we give them one of our thirteen booths in our consumption room. We show them where the harm-reduction supplies are and then allow them to cook the shot while we observe. Once they're done, they clean up and can spend some time in our Chill Out Lounge, Insite's "community space" for post-dose observation.

We can also offer clean, safer, medical-grade prescription opioids as a replacement for street drugs. One of the biggest causes of overdose deaths is the toxic drug supply. When I say "toxic drug supply," I don't mean it's toxic in the same way as, say, a poisonous berry. What I mean is that there's no quality control on the street. Fentanyl is so potent that even a couple of additional grains is the difference between overdosing or not. With fentanyl, people are incapable of judging their intake based on the potency and the mix of what they're buying on the street. So, we give our safer-supply participants a choice. They can access our prescription drugs or they can stick with their street drugs, and if they choose the latter, we can do spectrometer testing and tell them specifically what's in their supply. Then they can make an informed decision.

But we don't force anyone to do anything. It's all about relationships and having conversations. If we notice someone is overdosing regularly, we say, "Hey, we have this safer-supply program. It might work for you. It might not. But if you're interested, this is what we can offer." It's unfortunately a small sub-program currently, due to cost, but we're building it.

*At Insite, staff responds to emergencies not only on site, but also in the surrounding areas. Here, I display some of the common equipment used in off-site overdose response.*

One of the great things about Insite is that it's a place to come in and feel safe and be seen as a human being. A lot of the people we see have felt dehumanized in health care settings, so we want Insite to feel like their place, where they can just talk. It could be about anything—music, politics, the neighbourhood, etc. Frankly, it's not just for them. That one-on-one human interaction makes for my best days, when what I do doesn't feel like work, it feels like connection.

Since opening in 2003, we have had more than 4 million visits to our site and zero overdose deaths. Zero. But we don't have the funding to be open twenty-four hours a day, which means some of our participants have died off-site. And when we hear about it, it gets really heavy. These are people we have probably seen more regularly than our own families. It's easy to start beating ourselves up, asking, "What more could we have done?" We get angry with policymakers who don't make harm reduction, updating antiquated drug policy, and treatment options a priority, even with the sheer level of carnage on the street.

In October 2021, my brother passed away from an overdose. He was thirty-seven years old. He had a really long, clean run, but in that recovery phase, he was at high risk for overdose. He knew he could come to Insite for a safe injection—he'd been a participant in the past—but maybe he felt some stigma because I worked here. Or maybe there was a bit of arrogance. Maybe he thought, "Oh, it'll be fine. I remember my dosing. I remember how much I should be using."

But what's on the street today is not what was out there two or three years earlier. My brother's story is not unique, which is the saddest part. His life and death guide a lot of my work, and my philosophy about how I engage with users. They are our family, friends, and neighbours. We're trying to keep them alive.

*When we think of government, we often think of faceless politicians
in a capital city far away. But it's municipal governments that
have the closest ties to the people. When garbage collection is a
problem, or sewers or roads, you don't call Ottawa, you call your
councillor or the mayor. They make sure your town runs as it should.
Like Jennifer Handley, the mayor of Nanton, Alberta, thirty-five
minutes south of Calgary. Nanton has a population of about 2,200
people, and Handley is in her second four-year term as mayor.*

◆

# THE MAYOR
## Jennifer Handley

How does a small town differ from a big city? There are many ways. But here's one: If you're ever in Nanton, you may run into me, the mayor, when you least expect it. Not at city hall. I don't even have an office there. But on 21st Avenue at a restaurant called The Buzz. It's owned by my husband, Geoff, and from time to time, the server carrying the order of chicken quesadilla and bacon Caesar salad is me—Her Worship, Madam Mayor.

Being the mayor isn't even my full-time job. I'm a real-estate agent, which is what brought me to Nanton fifteen years ago. I was living in Calgary but showing houses in Nanton when I stumbled across a property that I liked. I told my husband about it over dinner, and he said, "Well, we should go take a look at it." I was born and raised in Calgary, a city girl through and through, but we liked the pace in Nanton. We felt like we could just breathe. So we made a low offer, but it was accepted. It was all very impulsive, but we have never regretted the move.

At the time, we had two young kids, and I was volunteering for everything, so it was easy to get to know people in town. I started planning real-estate events—like a parade of garage sales—to bring potential buyers to Nanton, and made more of a name for myself as a local real-estate agent. In 2013, five years after we moved, the town council asked me to do a presentation about how homes were selling. I remember being so nervous because I'd never met a mayor or a councillor, and those were impressive titles to me. The presentation went well, but when I came home, I told my husband, "No one looks like me on council. There was just one woman there and nobody under forty."

That's how I got it into my head that I could run for council. I knew the next municipal election was just three months away, but my gut was twisted up about it. I was thirty-two. My kids were just six and eight years old. Did I really want to put myself out there? Apparently, I did. The more I thought about it, the more it felt like the right thing to do. I had something to offer, so I threw my hat into the ring.

In Nanton, there were no party politics. Everyone ran independently, and the six candidates with the most votes became councillors. Thirteen people ran, and I came out at the very top.

We have a good mix of people living in Nanton. Some have been here for generations, but a good number have come from the city and are looking for a simpler lifestyle. We are primarily a ranching and farming community, but there's also a very artistic group here. Some are semi-retired and retired, others commute to Calgary or split their workweek between Calgary and Nanton.

When I was a councillor, I used to say that only a retired person could be mayor because there was no way a working person would have enough time for the job. But in 2017, when the sitting mayor decided not to run again, I persuaded myself that as a self-employed woman, I had a flexible schedule and could balance everything. And so, I ran for mayor—and won.

After I won, I found out I was right. A big-city mayor has a full-time job dealing with the police, the fire department, garbage collection, potholes, and on and on. For a small-town mayor, it's pretty much all the same, just on a smaller scale. While I'm never really off the job, I spend about fifteen hours a week, give or take, doing actual town work in addition to at least two four-hour council meetings each month.

This is partly because the RCMP, who are federally and provincially managed, do our policing, though I work with them to set local priorities.

Nanton has about twenty staff members, so it's important to understand our capabilities and our limitations, especially when it comes to our town budget. We have a volunteer fire department that we have to equip. We pay for garbage collection and recycling, water and wastewater treatment, and all town services like parks and recreation.

When it comes to fostering development and making the town attractive to businesses, we usually play the long game, not expecting to see instant results.

Our biggest issue is taxes. Our small-town taxes are higher than they are in Calgary simply because our smaller population means we have fewer taxpayers and fewer resources to pay for the same services and major infrastructure (albeit on a smaller scale) than the city. Property taxes are just as visible in small towns as they are in a big city. People are used to seeing income taxes taken off their paycheques, but property taxes are different—that's money taken from their bank accounts every month. So, taxpayers want greater accountability from politicians using that money.

And so I try to communicate with residents about how we spend their money. I include a letter in the tax bill, explaining that decreasing our spending by 1 percent amounts to only $21,000 in savings. The average taxpayer might save $12 a year. In other words, it would take a massive amount of cuts to make a significant dent in their property taxes. And there's not many areas we can cut—most of our spending is in infrastructure like garbage, roads, water, and sewage, and we need those. The only significant cut we could make would be to close the recreation centre, but no one would want that.

When people suggest we lower the council wages, I remind them that those costs are also miniscule. As mayor, I make $16,000 a year. Our councillors make $10,000 a year. Simply put, we are not doing this for the money; we are doing it because we care about our community. And there has to be some compensation for our time.

Women in politics often have a rough time of it, and it's no different for me, even in a small town. When I was a councillor, people seemed to be reasonably comfortable with me, but when I ran for

*My mom, Cathy Flanagan, with me at the
Alberta Municipalities award ceremony, where I
received the Queen's Platinum Jubilee Medal.*

mayor, people would come right out and say, "It's okay for a woman to be a councillor, but we need a strong man to be mayor. Someone who can really take control." Even some women would say that to me. All I could say in reply was, "I'm sorry you feel that way, and if I'm elected, I hope I can make you proud."

Even today, people sometimes come to council to ask a question, and they look right past me to my male colleagues for a response. I'm soft-spoken, so maybe people assume I can't be effective. When I was first elected as mayor, I went to a meeting of the mayors and reeves of

Southern Alberta, and an MLA came up to me and said, "How's the prettiest mayor in Southern Alberta?" I was a little shocked. I thought, "He thinks that's all it took to get elected? It's not my substance? It's not my experience? It's my blonde hair and blue eyes?"

I'm a perpetual people pleaser—that's just who I am. Once I realized that I could never make everyone happy, I became much more effective in my role. When I was a councillor, I could walk around town almost anonymously. But now if I go to a restaurant, the doctor's office, or my kids' school, someone is bound to stop me with a complaint or a question. Why weren't the garbage cans cleaned at the park on the weekend? Why does my water taste a certain way? We have big debates about gopher control. Some say we've got too many gophers. Others say we can't get rid of them—they love watching gophers. Everybody has an opinion. When I was elected mayor, I stopped collecting my mail from the post office because I was constantly stopped, and I wasn't always ready to have those conversations. Anywhere else I go, I'm prepared for questions. It's just part of my life.

COVID was an especially difficult time for Nanton. The town was split over the health and safety decisions being made. We tried to take direction from the provincial government, but when there were inconsistencies in their messaging, our citizens expected Council to step in and take positions. It was a lose-lose proposition for us nearly every time. For example, we had to close the hockey rink and playgrounds for a time, and we got a lot of pushback on that.

One of our municipal elections coincided with the peak of COVID frustration. The town was badly divided, and people were looking for political leaders to blame. As a result, the election campaign was quite toxic. When it was over, even though I won, I really didn't feel like celebrating my victory.

One of the good things to come out of COVID was a surge in small businesses. Some entrepreneurs noticed that people weren't leaving town as much, and they opened businesses to serve them. Some parts of town pretty well shut down, but we found a way to continue implementing the council's strategic plan we had created when I became mayor, which I'm very proud of. We also wanted to make sure people stayed active but safe, so we created a free disc golf course for all ages at one of our largest parks. Now it's a massive tourist draw that has helped our businesses. I'm very happy we could do that.

It's rewarding to see the results of projects that I have been working on for years. Like urban chickens and urban bees. We've got big property lots in town, so I thought it would be a good idea if we enabled people to have chickens and beehives within town limits for personal use only. The council was split down the middle. We did surveys and found the town was also split down the middle. Ultimately, it took three years, but we passed the bylaw four votes to three.

What keeps me going is I believe in the work. I know I've got the skill set and the tools to be effective. When the work bears fruit, that's what keeps me putting my signs on people's lawns at election time. In the end, even with all the opinions, I love the closeness of a small town and how every single person can make a major difference.

*Churches and other spiritual buildings have long been gathering places. No matter what you might believe, these buildings are points of connection and community and that's due in large part to the people who run them. People like Archdeacon John Clarke, the rector of St. Paul's Church, an Anglican church in Charlottetown, PEI, since July 2004.*

---

# THE PRIEST

## John Clarke

Some people ask if being a priest is a job or a calling. The Church says I don't get a paycheque, I get a stipend, but it looks and feels like a paycheque, and there are taxes taken off. That implies that it's a job, though perhaps not in the traditional sense. But a calling? I've always shied away from that language. How can I be sure what God wants of us? Or of me? I believe God calls on us all to be good people, to be people of love and to be people of faith. I'm responding to God's call to be a faithful person, by having a role in the church.

One role I have is that of rector of St. Paul's Church, where I do the traditional job of a priest, and another is as an archdeacon in the diocese of Nova Scotia and Prince Edward Island, where I assist the bishop in a variety of ways. As an archdeacon, I'm a troubleshooter, the first person sent in when there's an issue within a parish. If a rector decides to retire or move, I'm part of the process to find a new one. If a rector falls ill, I find people to lead worship on Sundays, and I help out with weddings and funerals. If there's personality conflict among clergy or between clergy and their parishes, I'm often asked to figure out the right solution. About 20 percent of my time is dedicated to this work, which I enjoy.

But I love working in my parish, doing weddings, baptisms, funerals, and Sunday services. And there's more to all of that than people think.

For example, the wedding is just the half hour we're in church and we say the blessings and attend a party afterwards. But marriage is more than that. Before the wedding, I usually sit down with couples three or four times to talk about their attitudes and expectations for marriage. Most couples have been living together for a long time before they get married, so they already have a good idea of the need for caring and fidelity, but it's good to consider some questions. How will the in-laws react? Will there be children? What are the religious expectations?

I especially enjoy weddings when I've had a chance to get to know the couple, but that isn't always the case. Sometimes they just show up at my door. Sometimes they've come home to PEI to get married, but the prep work was done by a priest in another part of the country. I don't really have a sense of connection with them. But when I know the couple, perhaps even as teenagers, I find those weddings joyful. There is a real sense of celebration in the community.

Baptisms, like weddings, have an educational component. Some people think baptism has to be done as soon as possible, or the child will end up in hell, but that's not one of the teachings of the Church. Anyone can be baptized—young or old. So, I talk to parents—or the child if they're older—about the meaning of baptism for the family and what the expectations are of Christian people.

When I was training to be a priest, the thing I feared most was performing funerals. But what I have found over the years is that most of the time they're not difficult. I get together with the immediate family to plan the service, including the readings and hymns they want and who they want to participate. That time gives me a chance to provide pastoral care, to talk about the individual who has passed away and the family's relationship with them. Sometimes people are open to these conversations, and sometimes they are not. It's difficult to be with somebody in the immediate moment of their grief. But when I take a

*Here I am with my family on the night I was ordained. From left to right: my brother, Rev. Dr. Jody Clarke; my mother, Diana; my father, Joe; me; and my sister, Penny.*

step back and think about the journey they've been on, from spouse to caretaker to griever, and then, eventually, returning to a productive member of the church or society, it's an honour to walk that path with somebody.

In more than thirty years, I've handled all kinds of funerals. There are natural deaths after a long life, but there are also stillbirths, sudden deaths of very young people, suicides, and medically assisted deaths. These can be especially difficult, and sometimes I don't know what to say other than to acknowledge the deep pain that we're all experiencing.

The death of a loved one can cause a crisis of faith. Usually, people come through it, and either their faith remains intact or they're able to rebuild it. When that doesn't happen, I can't force them to find their way back. There's no special prayer or formula I can give them. All I can do is continue to love and be with them in the midst of their pain.

At St. Paul's, I also prepare and lead Sunday worship, picking hymns and scriptures and ensuring that there are people assigned to take on various roles like ushers, readers, and choir members. Since COVID, we've broadcast our services online, which involves organizing PowerPoint slides so people can watch and follow along. This means I need to be prepared well in advance. So, rather than say, picking a Eucharistic prayer that strikes me in the middle of the service and telling people to turn to page 165, I have to pick it on Tuesday morning so it can get into the slides.

Then there's the work that goes into preparing a sermon. The Anglican Church has a three-year cycle of readings, so the themes of sermons follow that pattern. But I don't very often write out my sermons, so I can't just go back three years and pull a whole sermon off the shelf. I do keep notes, and I do go back and look at those. Sometimes I can remember something of it, but sometimes the notes make no sense to me at all. I'm also a bit of a storyteller, but I make sure to let six or seven years pass before I repeat a story, and even then, I try to use it in a different context. This backfired on me once when I gave a sermon in Halifax, and wouldn't you know it, there was a parishioner from Charlottetown in the congregation. He immediately recognized the sermon, and he teased me that I was trying out my material at home before taking it on the road.

I have all kinds of parishioners. One of the attractive things about St. Paul's is our radical sense of inclusion. By that I mean that even an atheist or agnostic is welcome. We have parishioners who are regularly involved in the church who wouldn't describe themselves as believers. They like the church, like the community, like the singing, like the social justice issues we take on, and they are involved. I think it's a good thing for any organization to have a loyal opposition that will challenge us on all sorts of things, including our basic beliefs.

Personally, I've never really doubted God's existence. My doubts are usually around me and my abilities and whether I'm really the right person to carry out my duties. Some people think of clergy as high and mighty. I know clergy doesn't think of themselves that way. Most of my colleagues are very sensitive to criticism. Not because it hurts our egos. It goes deeper than that. If I hear, "Your sermon was too long today," I lie in bed that night worrying about that. I worry about the impact I have on everyone. Is there somebody who's not at church because of me? Every criticism, every failure, or every failure that I perceive, sits with me for a long time. I think of these doubts as dumbbells. I exercise with them, they build strength, and I'm able to work out whether God wanted me to do this or that or not. Still, I can't say that I've ever felt as though a course of action I've chosen is exactly what God wants me to do, but that's a key benefit of being part of a religious community. We have each other to check in with.

Parishioners come to me with their spiritual questions. "Am I way off base here, or is this something that God might want me to do?" I encourage that—a check-in with others on what God might be calling us to do. We all know who to ask if you want someone to just agree with you. But we also know that's not the right way to go. Everyone needs to find someone who will challenge us. I tell parishioners to do that, and that's what I try to do too.

When people hear I'm a priest, they often watch what they say around me. Cursing is the most obvious thing. When I was in Cape Breton, I used to go visit an old, retired fellow who lived on a very narrow street that led down to the wharf. He often had people dropping in, and he would never introduce me because he wanted his visitors to get in a few really good curse words before he'd say, "Oh, by the way, this is my good friend, the Anglican priest." Then his guest would turn red and start apologizing. My friend found this very amusing, but I'm not particularly offended by cursing. If someone misuses the words Jesus Christ, I might give you a look, but even I've slipped a couple of good curse words into a sermon to make a point.

We curse because we're human. We also pray because we're human. Many people think that if they pray for something, it will happen, but prayer is a way to express love, especially when we pray for others. We want the best for them. I pray every day, but it's not formal prayer. Nothing written down. For example, when I go to the hospital to see if I have any parishioners there, I pray as I walk from my car to the front door that somehow, I can be present with whoever I see in a way that is helpful to them. That's really what my job is all about.

*There are tens of thousands of charities in Canada, and they all depend, to some extent, on the goodwill of ordinary citizens making donations. Meet Ken Mayhew, whose job is a challenging one. He fundraises for hospitals in the greater Toronto area, where he's the president and CEO of the William Osler Health System Foundation.*

◆

# THE FUNDRAISER

## Ken Mayhew

As a professional fundraiser for more than thirty-five years, I've become pretty good at hearing the word *no*.

I work for William Osler Health System Foundation, raising money for a large system of community hospitals in the greater Toronto area, specifically Brampton Civic, Etobicoke General, and Peel Memorial. When people connect with me, when they agree to see me, they know why I'm there. We're going to exchange pleasantries at first, get to know each other a bit, but before long, we're going to get to the part where I ask them to consider a donation. For those who are not predisposed to give, it's a brief exchange, but most are willing to have a longer conversation, even if their answer is no. People have all kinds of valid reasons not to give. Perhaps they support other worthy causes, or they have other priorities, or maybe they've got financial pressures, so it's just not the right time. None of that is unusual.

I meet people where they are. Maybe this week isn't the best time to talk about a donation, but next week will be. My role is to create the conditions for a person, a family, a corporation, or a foundation to feel comfortable in giving. People need to have a sense that a contribution, regardless of amount, will have impact, that it will make a meaningful difference.

That's true whether the donation is $2 a month or a large, transformational amount. What surprises some people is that those small gifts are as important as the big ones. Of course, I'm grateful for the huge donations that enable us to build an entire wing for a hospital, but it takes a community coming together for real success. In fact, the small donors provide the proof of concept—they often persuade the large donors to become involved. In other words, the people who can donate a sizeable sum want to know there's a large number of people who also believe in the cause and are willing to support it.

For example, 9,200 donors came together in a funding drive to help Etobicoke General Hospital, which is in an area of Toronto of modest social economic means. More than 800 of those people were our own physicians and staff. In addition to everything else they do for the hospital every day, they stepped up to say, "This is where I work. This is where I live. This is where I would take my family if they needed care. I want to do something." Those donations are relatively small, but in aggregate they show that giving begins at home. So when I talk to someone who might have the capacity to be a transformational donor,

I can tell them they're going to be part of a cause to which thousands of people are already contributing.

The way I look at donations is that people should give in their own way, at their own level. For one group or family, that can be a seven-, eight-, or nine-figure gift. For someone else, it may be a four-figure gift. For many people, giving $1,000 to a cause, or $1,000 a year for five years, would be the biggest donation they've ever given. It might literally involve some financial sacrifice, but I see it happen. People reach a point when they're ready. They ask themselves, "If not now, when?" I'm always inspired when someone who might be on a fixed income or might not have very much makes the greatest donation of their life to our hospitals. The gift I was truly humbled by was for $250 from someone I deeply admired and knew had to stretch to give it. The actual amount is frankly less material to me than the fact that they made the gesture. The most rewarding donation is the one that is transformational to the *donor*. It feels good when that happens.

People are motivated to give for so many different reasons. For some, it's a continuation of their family values. Maybe they were part of a religious group growing up, where giving is a form of tithing. For some, it's just what they do as part of their community. Others want to give because they've had some good fortune. And then there are those who have come through a life-or-death situation and want to pay it back to those who helped them. I do not convince people to give. My job is to professionally and ethically connect with those who seek to connect with us.

One of the questions I'm occasionally asked is why a hospital has to fundraise at all. In Canada, many people expect the government to pay for hospitals, and that's true—to an extent. It varies from province to province, but in Ontario, the government will pay 90 percent of the cost of construction for a hospital—billions of dollars to be sure—but for ongoing upgrades and equipment, the hospital has to find funding in the community. I think it's based on the notion that the public should have some skin in the game, that they should realize health care is not something to be taken for granted. Some hospitals might have a mega donor or two. Most are more like ours, where the funding gap is closed by donations from a lot of people, each doing a little bit.

Charitable fundraising is a competitive business. There are about 170,000 charities and nonprofits in Canada. At more than 8 percent of the country's GDP, it's comparable to the financial sector; or mining, oil, and gas; or the automotive industry. It's a massive industry, and there are only so many donor dollars to go around. Some individuals and some companies don't give to any causes. Others have specific societal priorities for giving, and I consider that in my approach. For example, the COVID pandemic raised awareness and concern about systemic inequality in access to health care and recovery resources. William Osler Health System was one of the epicentres of the pandemic because of the population we serve, which includes multi-generational households and those with precarious employment situations. So, a donation to our hospital aligned with corporations who are concerned about health care equity. It's a fit.

When it doesn't fit, I have to be honest about it. I have turned down donations because I couldn't meet the expectations of the donor. We're a community hospital that provides care to a huge number of people, but if someone wants to fund open-heart surgery, something we don't do, I send them to a hospital that does that procedure. Their contribution would be welcome here, and it would make a difference to us, but if they're set on that procedure, I refer them to somebody else. I've done that many times over the years.

*With my friend, philanthropist and champion of local health care Lois Rice.*

My job is to find those who are willing or are predisposed to support my cause. We know, for example, that if someone has no connection whatsoever to one of the Osler hospitals, the likelihood of them making a donation is remote. But there are moments in life when people become reflective. It could be a health crisis like cancer or heart disease. Or it could be the passing of a family member that leads people to want to help. If our hospitals were there for someone or their family at some critical juncture, they're more likely to be there for us.

We call that affinity to the cause.

And that happens relatively organically. For starters, we have patient confidentiality rules in Canada, so we do not have access to any records that would allow us to contact patients directly. What we do is nudge people when they cross our path. We have marketing materials within our hospitals. We have displays on our elevators. We have signage with the real stories of people who want to testify to the excellent care they received. That kind of thing encourages people to think about contributing. It happens several times a day, every day. People just drop by the office, knock on the door, and make a donation. They might say, "There's a nurse upstairs who helped my mom, and I'd like to show my appreciation." That's affinity to the cause.

When it comes to bigger donations, there can be a long period of negotiation before the gift is made. For example, the children of a mother who received end-of-life care at one of our hospitals wanted to honour her through a donation. They were very grateful for the care the hospital provided and wanted to help the unit that looked after their mother. When I met with them, they told me the heartwarming story of their mother's arrival in Canada, and how she had supported the family with her hard work. And then we discussed how we could recognize her life by naming something after her.

There's a wide range of options for big donations, but we do have a structured process to make sure that there's equity. Some people want to have a little story in the hospital newsletter about their donation or their family member. Others want a small reception. Some want their names on a wall. But many times, they want nothing at all. I remember a brother and sister who both left all they had to the hospital because we cared for their older sister when she was dying. They asked for nothing in return.

Fundraising is very personal for me. I once spent a week tapping into different parts of our community. On Tuesday, I was at a church talking to people. On Thursday, I was at a gurdwara, a Sikh temple, explaining my cause. On Friday, I was with the Portuguese community. On Saturday, I was at a mosque. And on Sunday, I celebrated the Chinese New Year. It was a great week because in a world that often feels so divided, I experienced an understanding, not just through words, but through deeds, that giving was important. I don't even re-call how much we raised—I don't think it was an enormous amount of money—but it was very rewarding to realize that people from all walks of life were united in common purpose: the need to have quality health care close to home.

I share that commitment. I want to ensure that my friends and col-leagues at the hospital, who are on the front lines dealing with patients and families every single day, have the resources they need to deliver the best care possible. I personally feel constant pressure to hold up my end. I don't think that fundraising is necessarily for the faint of heart. It takes persistence, and it takes drive. There are lots of days when, de-spite best efforts, the answer is no. But it's my calling, and I stick with it because the consequence of my work is significant, and things that are worthwhile are often difficult.

*I don't know about you, but the words "forensic biology" make me nervous. Not because I don't appreciate the value such a science can bring to society and to the country's courtrooms, but because it takes me back to my school days. To me, any kind of science class, with its complicated symbols and theories, gave me the jitters, convincing me I'd never get the grades. But not so for Valerie Blackmore. She's a forensic biologist, the cofounder and president of the Wyndham Forensic Group, based in Guelph, Ontario.*

◆

# THE FORENSIC BIOLOGIST
## Valerie Blackmore

Many people are surprised that private forensic biologists like me exist. And they think that my job is like what they see on TV. People assume that forensic work is done by scientists who work with the police or the government, but that is probably because police are responsible for criminal investigations. And while it's true that most criminal forensic testing work in Canada is done in government-run labs, there are many reasons why a private lab like ours at Wyndham Forensic Group is used.

Sometimes investigators want access to advanced services, cutting-edge technology, or a different level of service. Sometimes defence counsel needs to understand what the DNA evidence is against their client. Sometimes relatives of missing persons come to us, or unidentified human remains need to be examined.

It is also important to remember that there are two sides to our criminal justice system in Canada, and when a case goes to trial, both the Crown prosecutors and defence counsel want access to separate forensic experts. Without private forensic experts, there would be no mechanism for defence counsel to access independent testing for the other half of our justice system.

Private forensic experts work with more than just the police. I get requests from victims of crime or their family members who feel that more work could be done on a case. Perhaps someone has been sexually assaulted and is not sure if they want to contact the police and start a criminal investigation yet. Sexual assault complainants send their sexual assault evidence kits directly to our lab and ask me to tell them what kind of evidence was on their body so that they can then make important decisions.

The cases that I work on are extremely sensitive and emotional for the parties involved, but the role of a forensic scientist is to maintain objectivity. It is not because I don't care or understand how important the issues are, it is because that is how I can assist with criminal, civil, or regulatory matters. It's important to let our clients know that the evidence will speak for itself, and, when I become involved, I don't know if it will necessarily help their cause or get them the answer that they want, but I can help them understand what evidence exists and what that evidence means and doesn't mean. Everyone deserves answers—if there are answers to be had.

DNA testing is often the first thing everyone thinks of when it comes to forensic science. In fact, that's how I got into this field. When I was in graduate school doing breast cancer research, I was following the O. J. Simpson trial, which was on TV every day for many months. The DNA evidence against him was very powerful, but his defence team mounted a withering attack on the lab that did the testing, and we know how that turned out. I was using the same techniques in my research lab, and I became excited about the idea of applying the DNA

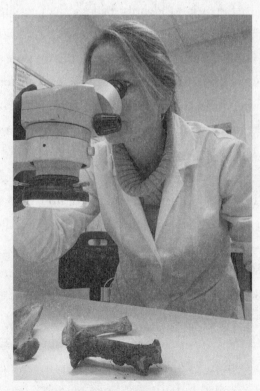

*In the lab, studying bone fragments*
*for DNA evidence.*

science and skills that I'd learned to forensic science. Around the same time in Canada, the Paul Bernardo case sparked an expansion of the Centre of Forensic Sciences, and I went to work there. Several years later, I started a private laboratory called Wyndham Forensic Group.

On occasion, I leave the lab to attend crime scenes, but it's not common. For example, if a police officer shot a civilian, an expert not associated with the police department or the police lab might be asked to also attend the scene. Generally, it is the police services who are responsible for securing a crime scene and they have highly trained individuals to collect evidence.

When evidence comes to our lab, maybe a piece of clothing or a weapon, the first step is to identify biological material. Is anything there, and what is it? Is it blood? Is it semen? Is it saliva? Is it a mixture of those bodily fluids? From there, we attempt to develop a DNA profile that can help identify who left the biological material. I usually know something about the crime—breaking and entering, shooting, sexual assault, robbery, drug dealing, homicide—and the context of the material I'm examining, such as where it was found and its possible relevance to the case. The police, prosecutors, or defence counsel may have a theory about the case, but it's not my job to support their theory. It's my job to use the scientific method and tell them what the science says, even if in some cases the science says nothing at all. Sometimes the DNA testing just isn't helpful. Sometimes there is no DNA on an item. Sometimes I go to court to explain the reasons why there might not be DNA on an item.

Even when the DNA results are exactly what the police or defence counsel want to hear, I don't know what the other evidence is in the case. When I'm called to testify in court, my job is not to convict or acquit anyone. That is the role of the judge or the jury. While I have confidence in my scientific results, the results are not always black and white. There are a lot of grey areas and I have to be able to communicate that sometimes there are still things unknown. Sometimes forensic testing just can't address the question at hand. For example, there could be too many people who have left DNA on a firearm, and picking one person out of that DNA mixture is impossible.

Testifying in court is part of the work. It can be challenging and there can be a lot of waiting and rescheduling. If I'm called by the Crown to provide evidence, then my evidence probably supports the prosecutor's case, and I might be explaining how the DNA profile on the evidence matches that of the accused. Then I'll be cross-examined by the defence counsel, whose job is to challenge that evidence. They may try to suggest I wasn't properly trained or that the results aren't reliable. But if I'm called to testify by defence counsel, my evidence probably supports the defence, in which case the Crown prosecutor will cross-examine me. Court is an adversarial process, but it isn't personal, and in our system, both sides use whatever strategy will maximize their chances of winning, and my testimony is simply a tool to that end.

In the end, I have faith in our justice system. In the courts, after all sides are heard, matters are properly resolved. I like that it's not up to me to decide a case. Instead, I am there to educate the court, remain objective, not pick sides—and, in fact, that is the oath that I take.

Not all forensic DNA testing involves a crime. Our lab also does a lot of testing to establish paternity or other relationships for private citizens and children's aid agencies, to settle estates, or for immigration purposes. When somebody in Canada wants to sponsor family members to immigrate, they may be required to do DNA testing to prove everyone they are sponsoring is indeed a relative. We also assist in identifying fallen Canadian soldiers. My colleagues and I also work in several different countries to help build and develop forensic science labs and train other forensic scientists.

My job is very rewarding because I work with not just police investigators and lawyers, but also with other scientists, international governments, and private citizens who have a lot riding on the test results. DNA, and the technology around it, matters to all of us, and I am honoured to help find meaningful answers to some of the most important questions in our society.

*The best way to experience a new place is to walk a mile in the shoes of someone who lives there. That's what Lesley Thompson is all about. She's the owner and the principal guide of MTL Detours, a company that offers walking tours in Montreal.*

◆

# THE TOUR GUIDE
## Lesley Thompson

I used to be one of those people who didn't want to take a guided tour. When I vacationed in another city, I didn't need a tour, or at least I didn't think I needed one. I had my guidebook and was content to let it lead me around. But what I've discovered is that there is more to be gained by connecting with the real people who live in the places that we visit, local people who have history, stories, and the inside scoop about what's going on.

At least, that's what I try to do as a tour guide in Montreal. Everyone thinks that summer is the busiest time for tours in Montreal, but September and October can also be very busy months. Cruise ships dock in the harbour, and other people come to the city to see the fall colours. But I think the *best* time to tour Montreal is in the winter.

In fact, that's how I started my tour business. Quite a few tourists come up here specifically to experience a Canadian winter and aren't afraid to bundle up and take a tour. It's actually a little magical to walk on the crunchy snow.

I remember a tour I led around Christmas one year. I had four people from the Dominican Republic with me who really wanted to see snow. Well, we don't always have a white Christmas. It's kind of hit and miss. And on this December day, all the Christmas decorations were up, but there was no snow on the ground.

I was just starting the tour, introducing myself in the square in front of the grand Notre-Dame Basilica, when the sky started to get all fluffy. Little flakes began coming down, then it got heavier and heavier, and the Dominicans cheered, "Snow. Snow. We're seeing our snow!" They were like little kids. It was just wondrous to them; some even had tears in their eyes. I'll never forget that.

While I have lived in Montreal my entire life, to become a licensed tour guide, I had to take an eight-month course from the Hotel and Tourism Institute of Quebec (ITHQ). For three evenings a week (plus some Saturdays), I was trained on how to speak and lead a group, as well as history, politics, art, architecture, urban planning, and more. With all these elements jammed into my brain, I had to pass a test to get my mandatory city permit, which I did, and I've been providing tours ever since.

Earlier in my career, I was a guide on a Hop-On Hop-Off bus. Those tours can be a lot of fun. I sat on the top deck of the bus at the back with my microphone, commentating on the sites as we went around. For people who want to get an overview, a bus tour is a great

*Talking to my tour group in the Place
d'Armes Square in Old Montreal.*

way to see a city. But if you want a more specialized, more concentrated look at a specific part of the city, that's what I offer.

My specialty is two-hour walking tours of Old Montreal. Each tour has a maximum of ten people. I don't want to have a big troop of people following behind an umbrella or a flag. It's not as personal, not as intimate. With only ten people on the tour, it gives everyone a chance to interact with me, to ask their questions. They're not standing in the back of a large group trying to hear me; I'm standing right in front of them. And when we're walking, we're right down in the thick of a neighbourhood and get to experience the local flavour. I cover the basics of Old Montreal, of course, the must-sees like Place Jacques

Cartier, Place d'Armes, Château Ramezay, Bonsecours Market. But I add many of my personal stories, things that bring it all to life. "My grandfather used to work for this company," "This is the Board of Trade, where my dad had his very first job as a teen," or "We used to have hot chocolate on the square here."

Some tourists come with a good understanding of Montreal and its history, but for most, the city is an entirely new place. Many people are surprised, for example, by how much English is spoken here. I start my tours with, "Bonjour, hi! Welcome, everybody. My name's Lesley. How are you?" And sometimes the first thing people will say to me is, "How come you don't have a French accent?" Then I explain that my ancestors came from England and Ireland, and that Montreal is a very multicultural city with a complex French-English past and present, but I also try to balance my tours with information about Indigenous Peoples and immigrant communities—not just focus on the French-English duality.

People want to have a good time. They don't want to be spoken to; they want to participate in an activity, interact with a local, and have fun. I'm not there to lecture them and give them a quiz at the end. They want to learn from somebody who's from here and who can tell them interesting things. What's that building? What's the story behind that sculpture? What's that square all about? What happened here? And in Montreal, they want to know why we're so famous for bagels and smoked meat! They want to hear about it from a real Montrealer, not just read about it. They won't remember all the dates I gave them, but they will remember the intriguing stories I told them.

I try to make my tours fun, interactive. I try to make everybody feel comfortable. Around 70 percent of my clients come from the United

States, and the rest are from elsewhere in Canada and farther flung international destinations, but everyone gets along and chitchats. It's not at all unusual for a little group of people to gel during the tour, and then go off for lunch together. I love seeing those connections.

Although there are the exceptions, most people are very engaged and enthusiastic, and I feed off their energy. I love it when people are really into the history, our culture, and ask questions. While I know a lot about the history of Montreal, it's not possible to know *everything*. If I get a sticky question and I don't know the answer, I tell them that I'll find the answer as soon as I get home. And I do. I'll look it up. I even send the person who asked an email with the answer. It's a constant learning process for me too.

I'm always researching, always looking for ways to make my tours even more interesting. I can know the year a building opened its doors and who the architect was, but if I start looking deeper, I can find out about a particular person who lived or worked in the building, and that's a story I can add. Facts are good, but stories are better.

Being a tour guide is a full-time job for me. There's a lot of work leading up to the tour. I plan our route carefully. There are so many possibilities, I have to consider the timing. I can't end a two-hour tour early, nor can I let it run late. Sometimes there are street closures, detours, and special events to contend with. I have to find a balance between walking and talking, and leave room to adjust when someone needs a bathroom break or someone has a mobility issue. In those cases, I try to stop and speak where there's a bench so someone who's having difficulty can sit down and rest. It takes lots of resourcefulness, adaptability, patience, and creativity.

When a tour ends, I don't just say, "Thanks, au revoir," and walk away. There's always time to hang out, take extra questions, and give recommendations for dining, shopping, and things to do in the city. My tours always include a personal touch—a tiny treat and a unique parting gift. I do photography for fun and I love sharing samples of my special Montreal shots with my guests.

When I get home after a day of tours, I still have the administrative side of my business to take care of, which includes maintaining my website so that it's searchable on Google, updating my tour calendar, answering emails, creating customized tours for special requests, doing research, and publishing social media posts.

But it's all worth it to do a job that's perfect for me and that allows me to connect with people and share the magic of my beautiful city.

*The average Canadian drinks about sixty litres of milk in a year. The next time you're in the grocery store, take a minute to think about how the milk you see got there. It started with a farmer, like David Wiens in Grunthal, Manitoba, about seventy-four kilometres south of Winnipeg. His farm is one of about 10,000 in Canada, which combine to produce about 10 billion litres of milk every year.*

---

# THE FARMER
## David Wiens

As a third-generation farmer, I've got farming in my blood. My grandparents bought my farm in Grunthal, Manitoba, in 1926, and passed it down to my father and uncle, who passed it on to me and my brother. I was born and raised on this farm. I know there are a lot of other easier ways to make a living, but I have an attachment to the cows and to the land—and not just any land, *this* land.

When my grandparents purchased the farm, it was a quarter section or 160 acres. The farming equipment in the 1920s was not as efficient as it is today. There were tractors, but most of the work on the farm was still done by people or animals such as horses and mules, so 160 acres was about as big as a farm could be and still be manageable.

Today, I farm about 2,000 acres and milk about 230 to 240 cows. By Canadian standards, that's slightly above the average-sized dairy farm. In the United States, a dairy farm with fewer than a thousand cows is considered small.

Having lived all my life on this farm, I've seen how things have changed over time. My grandfather could not even have imagined what the farm looks like today. Even my father, who died in 2002, would have considered the things we do now as science fiction. There were some automated milking systems in his time, but they were thought to be experimental. We still brought the cows in ourselves and hooked them up to milking machines two to three times a day, which was doable when we had a smaller herd. I remember we used to fill out farm surveys where one of the questions was, "Is it essential to have computer technology?" At one point, I would have said, "No, not really. It's nice to have, but we don't really need it." Today, with more than 200 cows, we would not be able to function without it. (For reference, my father started with twenty cows in 1967.)

In 2008, my brother and I had to build a new barn, so we went to Quebec where they had some automated milking systems, and we came away impressed and enthused. These systems maximize milk production of an existing herd, which means we wouldn't have to increase the number of cows on our farm to increase revenue. Automation also prioritizes the cows' welfare—there are fewer infections, and the process of milking is always predictable, which makes for happier and healthier cows in general.

We were convinced. So, when we built our new barn, we installed a milking area in the centre with four automated stations. When the cows are ready to be milked, they walk in, anytime of the day or night, and the system washes and dries every teat individually, then it picks up the milking cups, attaches each one separately, and milks the cow. When it's done, it withdraws the milking cup.

Every cow wears a transponder, so the system identifies the cow, and it knows everything about her—its length, the exact structure of the udder, and so on. There's even a camera so we can see what the cow is doing. The system records the production not just from each cow, but from each teat. The first thing I do when I go into the barn is check the report. I can see exactly what's happened. If, for some reason, a cow hasn't come to milk, or if a cow's production was suddenly lower than expected, that would be flagged, and I could follow up to see if there's an issue of some kind.

As a modern farmer, my well-being is directly tied to the cows' well-being. And I know a lot more than I used to with this system.

Even when a cow comes through the automated milking station for the very first time, it's a calm and relaxed setting. It's very seldom that a cow is upset or uncomfortable. They learn the routine from each other. I think it took we humans longer to adapt to the new system than it took the cows. They didn't have to figure out how it all worked. It just worked for them. It helps that they get a treat of rolled grain corn while they're milked, so that makes them want to come back again and again. When I go into the stalls to clean them out, the cows are very quiet. While I'm putting down fresh bedding, they're very comfortable, unfazed by my presence.

On average, a cow will get milked three times in a twenty-four-hour period in our setting. The system is set up so a cow can't come through more than once in six hours. If she decides that she's going to try to come through after four hours, the gate swings in such a way that she's diverted back to the stalls area, where she can choose to eat, drink, or lie down. Sometimes a cow will just stand there for a while, wanting to go to the milking area. But they move off soon enough when they realize the milking gate will not open for them.

It's not just the milking that's automated. The cows can decide when to self-groom too. We set up foot baths for the cows to walk through, which is good for their hooves. We also have big round brushes the cows can use to groom or scratch an itch. They look a bit like car-wash brushes, but for cows. When the cow touches the brush, it starts to spin, and the cow is groomed in all the hard-to-get-at places.

There's also an automated manure scraper that cleans the alleyways where the cows walk. And there's an automated feeding system. Food is put out automatically eight times in a twenty-four-hour period, so cows receive fresh feed, which they love, for each small meal.

All the automation means the cows live on their own schedules. There's never a rush to the feed bunk, to be milked, or anywhere. Everything just happens all the time. Some cows are night owls, so they'll be hanging out by the milking system at night, while others are already lying down in their favourite stall.

If the milking system ever breaks down, I get an immediate warning that something is wrong, and I go to the barn to try to see what the problem is. Occasionally it's a software issue that I can't handle, but usually it's something that can be quickly corrected. If there's a downside to automation compared to the old milking system, it's that if something broke down while people were milking, we were right there to deal with it. Now something can happen when a cow is being milked at three a.m. I've got to get on a problem right away because

I can't have one of the units not working for six or seven hours. I'm always on duty.

Normally, I call it a day at about eleven p.m. I spend the last two hours of my work in the barn, redistributing the bedding, cleaning things, checking the cows. Right now, we're in the process of installing waterbeds for them—actual water beds that we put straw bedding on top of. Cows like to lie down for long stretches of time, so it's smart to invest in their comfort. A comfortable cow lives longer and produces better. It's also why we have rubber floors in the alleys of the barn, so the cows are not walking on concrete. A veterinarian comes in every couple of weeks to make sure the herd is healthy.

Many dairy farms also grow crops. On my farm, we grow mostly alfalfa, corn, barley, and wheat. About 70 percent of our land is used to grow feed for the cows. It has to be carefully planned, with the help of an agronomist—an advisor who specializes in the study and care of crops and soils. We have to rotate our crops so as not to deplete the soil of its nutrients. The planning is done in the winter, so that we can get out onto the land as soon as possible in the spring, to start putting in the crops. In the fall, we do most of the harvesting.

We live by the weather. I've seen some years that were so wet we had to wait to harvest the corn crop until December, when the ground was frozen enough to carry the weight of the combine and other equipment. Other years, we get it all done in October. The weather impacts the quality and quantity of the feed, and that in turn will impact the cows' production for the year. In a wet year, I get huge volumes of feed, but the quality is poor, and I have to buy expensive supplements for the cows. In a drier year, there tends to be better quality, but less of it. If we could control the weather, we would have a perfect balance. But that's not ours to have.

If there happens to be extra crop after feeding our herd, we sell it to others. The one crop we always sell in its entirety is wheat. We grow a milling wheat so we can harvest the straw for the cows' bedding, but the grain is more valuable to other farmers. In fact, we need more straw than we can possibly grow. So we make arrangements with grain farmers in our area. We sell them our wheat; they sell us the straw that's left on their fields. That's why it's good to have a good mix of different farms in the same area.

No matter what is happening with my crops, the cows need care every day of the year. It doesn't matter how busy the planting season is or the harvesting season is, I always have the cows to look after.

Canada has a government-regulated supply management system for dairy, eggs, and poultry that controls the amount of food produced and the price farm staples are sold for. There are critics of the system, but for dairy farmers, it offers market and price stability and keeps

*On my farm in Manitoba with part of the herd.*

underpriced imports from being dumped into our market. Before the supply management system was put in place more than fifty years ago, farmers with perishable products were subject to the whims of the market. And the market was very local back then. Farmers had formed cooperatives to sell and process their milk, but they wanted to work on the provincial and even the national level on important issues like overproduction or underproduction, which lead to milk waste or having to feed it to pigs.

Supply management allows farmers to receive a stable income for their work. We feed our families and our fellow Canadians. And we stay in business, and we, in turn, keep a lot of other people in business—veterinarians, equipment suppliers, truck drivers, agronomists, and more. It's different in the U.S. They don't have a supply management system, and when the farmers struggle, the government has to bail them out to keep milk in the stores.

A few years ago, a group of farmers from Indiana came to visit, and I was telling them about the economic realities of how I ran things, and one of them shook his head and said, "We just could not do that at home because we don't have the stability in our market. I can't make long-term investments on my farm to make things better, because I don't know where prices are going to be in a year or two." Supply management brings stability and predictability to our farms. We can invest with more confidence over a long period of time.

Farming is a business. A farmer must have business acumen because they have to deal with debt, mortgages, and business plans just to operate the farm. But I don't think of myself as a businessman. I'm still very much a farmer whose first priority is my cows and my crops. While it's not as physically hard as it was when I was a boy, I'm still in the barn at eleven p.m., cleaning up a stall as a cow licks me. Most years, I work seven days a week and only take a week's vacation, but dairy farming is what I know and it's what I love. It's a way of life that I believe reflects values that are important in our society. I'm giving Canadians locally produced milk, cheese, butter, and yogurt, while caring for the land and caring for the animals.

*Knowledge creates possibilities. It opens doors. Universities are one of the key places to foster that knowledge. Dalhousie University, one of fifteen research universities in Canada, is the only one in Atlantic Canada. Boasting upwards of 20,000 students, Dalhousie offers more than 4,000 courses and 180 degrees in twelve undergraduate, graduate, and professional faculties. Deep Saini is the president.*

◆

# THE UNIVERSITY PRESIDENT
## Deep Saini

There was a time when universities were known as ivory towers, and perhaps the president of a university was thought of as the prime occupant of that tower. But I'm determined to change that idea.

Education is transformative, and it has taken me around the world. For that, I owe my father. Growing up in Punjab, India, in the 1920s, my father was the youngest son of a sugarcane farmer, and his family needed him to help in the fields. But one day, when his father—my grandfather—sent him to the village on an errand, he walked by a small elementary school, newly opened, and lucky for him, the teacher was handing out candy and books. My father couldn't resist. He went inside, and that first day of school changed his life forever, setting him on a path toward education.

When I was growing up, my father encouraged me and my three brothers to prioritize academics over all else, including athletics, because he knew the value of education. I went on to university, and I completed my bachelor's and master's of science in botany in India. From there, I went to Australia, where I studied for my PhD in plant physiology, and then Canada for my postdoctoral research fellowship at the University of Alberta. Canada became my home.

It wasn't just us boys who my father wanted to succeed. Throughout my childhood, he welcomed extended family members into our home and helped them pursue their education and careers. He had a phenomenal impact, thanks to the teacher who encouraged him to come to school. My father took me and my brothers to meet that teacher, and I was inspired how this one man changed the course of so many lives. After I finished my fellowship in Alberta, I took a variety of professor and leadership roles at universities across Canada—and a stint as the vice-chancellor and president of the University of Canberra—before becoming the president and vice-chancellor of Dalhousie University in 2020.

For anyone, but especially a young person, knowledge opens doors. It's one of the very few quantities in our world that multiplies when given away. Working to expand knowledge, whether it is through teaching and learning or through research, is ultimately what the president of a university is responsible for.

I call myself "the walking president." I often get out of my office and randomly walk around the campus, or stand in the Tim Hortons line even when I don't need a coffee, just to be able to connect with people. I try to go to as many student functions and activities as I can. It could be a club or a sporting event. Even if it's just ten or fifteen minutes, I do my best to show up. And I do the same sort of thing with the faculty and staff. Since my own education is in plant biology research, I get great pleasure walking into the labs because I understand what they're doing and am interested in their work. Dalhousie is a large organization, so it's not easy to keep up with everybody, but if two people who meet me each tell two other people, "I met the president and this is what he's like," then that's six people who may have a better understanding of what our goals are at Dalhousie.

Part of my job is to tear down the notion that we're an ivory tower once and for all. To that end, we've also worked hard to blur the line between where our campus ends and the city begins. Our sports complex accepts public membership. Our arts centre is the biggest performing arts centre in Atlantic Canada and is used as much for community events as university events. We have multiple dentistry clinics throughout the city. We also have a legal aid clinic. We're all about fostering greater community.

A university president is almost like being the conductor of a very complex orchestra. The key players in the orchestra are the members of my executive, including two vice presidents who are responsible for what constitutes the core, interconnected missions of the institution— teaching and learning on one side, and research and scholarship on the other. Dalhousie is a place for a very high level of intellectual experience, right from the undergraduate days. We can't be a good research university without paying attention to academics, but we need strong research to influence the quality of teaching at the institution. Other members of the executive deal with finances, infrastructure, fundraising, human resources, and government relations.

I work at the strategic level but am fully aware of the on-the-ground operations. In other words, I don't have to play the violin or the flute, but I must know how it is played, when somebody is not playing in concert with others, and when somebody is off-key. I defer day-to-day operations to the provost, while making sure that the strategy I have articulated to the team is being carried out harmoniously across the university. We are such a multi-activity institution, I make sure that the dots remain connected all the time and keep an eye on everything because ultimately, when something goes wrong, the buck stops with me.

I spend a lot of time with government, from deputy ministers to ministers, and I'm in the premier's office any chance I get. Government has always been important for universities, but it is becoming important in a new kind of way. In the past, governments provided their part of the funding and then let the universities do their thing. Increasingly, governments want to intervene and take part in how their money is spent. While their intentions are not bad, they don't always know how the university works.

For example, technology is booming in Atlantic Canada, but there was a dire shortage of computer scientists, and it was preventing even greater success in the industry. A university has a social responsibility to participate in the economic and social uplift of the region in which we operate. So, we expanded the size of our computer sciences programs and increased the number of students, but the number of faculty hadn't gone up. We had, by far, the highest ratio of students to professors in a major university that trains computer scientists. The typical range is 30 or 35 to 1; ours was 58 to 1.

So, we engaged with the government. We explained why we couldn't train more computer scientists to continue to fuel industrial growth here, and after a year-long conversation, convinced them to fund the hiring of more professors. We even agreed that for every dollar they put in, we'd put in a dollar from our internal sources. The result was that we doubled the size of our faculty in computer sciences and can now teach more students. Today, Dalhousie trains about 90 percent of the computer scientists in Nova Scotia and well over 50 percent in Atlantic Canada.

Another role I have is chief storyteller. People often prefer to talk to the president than to a fundraising professional, so I take a very active and leading role in our fundraising initiatives. I make speeches to our stakeholders so they're aware of the overall strategy of the institution. But a lot of the work happens in one-on-one conversations and relationship building. Our approach to fundraising at Dalhousie is that we ask people to give not to Dalhousie but through Dalhousie. For example, someone may have a special reason for wanting to see a cure for cancer, but they don't have a lab in which cancer research can be done. We do.

That's part of storytelling, and much of that happens with people who have already given to Dalhousie or are alumni, but sometimes it's with others who may never have given to the university. For example, we received a gift of $8 million from someone in Vancouver who had no previous connection to us. The donor was passionate about conservation, and when he heard about what we do in the area of ocean studies, he told us he wanted to help us create a centre for marine biodiversity. If I can tell a compelling story, sometimes that produces magic.

A lot of my day is structured. I have many meetings, but I always leave time for reading, writing, and meditation, so I can mentally be ready for whatever comes next, which could be anything. One moment, I could be talking with our athletic director who's concerned about why our hockey team is not performing well. The next moment, I could be talking with a potential Nobel laureate who's upset that his lab is not properly equipped. Then I could get a call from a government minister who says we haven't delivered on some target that they expected us to. And then at midnight, someone could be knocking on my door at home because a bunch of students are having a noisy party three blocks away, and they expect me to shut it down (which I can't do).

The *raison d'être* for any university is the students.

*Meeting students at one of Dalhousie's welcome receptions.*

If you take the students out, and we did just research, then we would be no different from the National Research Council. Students make us a university, and so our number one responsibility is to provide them with a well-rounded education so they can be effective citizens for the country and the world. Every university administrator is also mindful that more and more students are encountering mental health challenges, and I'm no different. It's important we address these issues so that our students can flourish.

While I worry about the students, they are the very best part of my job. The happiness I see in their faces, the sense of fulfillment I feel when I award them their degrees on convocation day is the reason why I do what I do. When a student breaks protocol and walks up behind a professor to give them a hug, or when families want to take pictures with me after the ceremony, I'm reminded that university isn't just about education, it's about connection. The feeling is impossible to beat.

## Postscript

*As of April 2023, Deep Saini is the principal and vice-chancellor of McGill University—also a publicly funded research university—where he continues to serve society through research and educational initiatives.*

*I've covered a few royal weddings, right back to Charles and Diana in 1981. I was always amazed at the thousands of organizers involved in every aspect, trying to make sure the heavily publicized hitch went off without a hitch. No comment on how that eventually worked out for some of the royals. Here at home, things happen on a much smaller scale, but wedding planners have become big business, and for many young couples (and their parents), they are an essential part of the big day. Wedding days are often full of tension, and it's the wedding planner's job to make all that go away.*

---

# THE WEDDING PLANNER

## Andrea Hounsell

Ever since I can remember, I have been obsessed with love stories. There's nothing more romantic than when two people find each other and commit to building a life together, and weddings are a celebration of their love in front of the people who matter most. It's arguably one of the most important days of their lives. It can be stressful to plan the day, but as a wedding planner, it's my job to manage not only the logistics of the day but also the stress of everything so the couple can enjoy their day and stay in their love bubble. That's my goal.

As much as I love weddings, I didn't intend to become a wedding planner. Growing up in Newfoundland, I studied music at Memorial University, then began giving private lessons while also gigging at weddings on the side. But I'd always been interested in interior design, and when I looked into a correspondence course at New York's Sheffield School, I saw they had just launched a wedding and event planning course. Immediately, the light bulb went off. I could combine my love of weddings with my love of design.

Wedding planners go back to the sixteenth century, but it's obviously changed over the years, and even in the last few years. At one time, the couple lived at their respective parents' houses until their wedding, and the bride-to-be planned the celebration with her parents over a few months, and then the couple would move in together post-wedding. Today, most people who get engaged already live together, and may have kids, and they're in no hurry to seal the deal and may wait a year or a year and a half so they can plan the perfect wedding day.

That's where I come in. After I completed my certification, I began my own wedding planning business in St. John's. The first lesson I learned about planning weddings here is that you have to be prepared for any weather situation. Here on the Rock, nearly every couple wants an outdoor ceremony, with the beautiful ocean water and rock cliffs in the background. It's the first question I get asked, and I can understand why. Our province boasts some of the most dramatic natural backdrops. But as an islander born and bred, I know how fickle the weather can be, and so I always have a backup plan.

Early in my career, I was working with a very sweet couple whose wedding was planned for early September 2010 at a local golf course. Their guest list was for 200 people, and they had a big budget, the biggest I had been involved with to that point, so I felt quite a bit of pressure to get things right, including the décor for the outdoor ceremony.

As it happened, their wedding fell on the day Hurricane Igor arrived, one of the worst storms ever to hit Newfoundland. The wind was roaring at about 170km/hr. There was no way we could put up a tent in those conditions, so I had to tell the couple their "perfect" setting wasn't going to be.

Then I went into planning mode. I came up with two options for the couple, so they would still be in control and know that their day was still going to work out. We moved the ceremony indoors, where the reception was going to take place. We set up a drape as the backdrop for the ceremony and shifted all the pre-set dinner tables behind it. After the ceremony, we arranged for the guests to return to the lobby for forty-five minutes of cocktails, giving us time to reset the entire room for the guests, many of whom were still attending despite the weather. I knew the night before that some staff wouldn't be able to get to the venue, so I was on the phone calling all of my friends and family, asking them to come out to help for forty-five minutes. And they did. That's often the beauty of weddings—they bring people together.

In the end, the couple was thrilled with how their day went. We succeeded in making the guests feel that they were still just going to a wedding and experiencing the couple's love story. They weren't worried about what was going on outside. The hurricane even knocked out the power for a while. The groom's father got on the phone to ask some people he knew to drop off generators, and before you knew it

*All set for a reception at the Delta Hotel in St. John's.*

we had three or four of them. That's a real Newfoundland thing—people show up for each other.

I see my job as making the journey from "I said yes" to "I do" easier. And in a small place like St. John's, Newfoundland, setting the date is often dictated by venue availability and vendor availability. In a bigger place, there are more choices for talented wedding vendors like hair stylists and makeup artists, who offer a range of rates. Not here. Vendors and venues book events three or four years in advance, which is why couples come to me. They can feel overwhelmed by all the little details and decisions. They don't know which florist is good, which bakery is reliable, which DJ is charging reasonable rates, which caterer is easy to work with. Trying to research everything is a full-time job, and what I offer is my knowledge, experience, and my time—I can do the running around, collecting quotes, negotiating contracts. The clients still make all the decisions, but I'm the insurance policy guaranteeing that nothing is overlooked or slips through the cracks. I make sure the invitations go out on time, that you have the best team with you on your wedding day, and the couple stays on budget. Besides the weather, the budget may be the most important part of my job.

The most common misconception about hiring a wedding planner is that everything will be more expensive when I enter the picture. In my very first call with prospective clients, I let them know that it's part of my job to make sure that if they have a budget in mind, then they stay at that price point. I'm not going to recommend a $10,000 photographer if they only have a $12,000 wedding budget. I'm only going to show them things that I think they're going to love within their price range. So I don't add to the budget, I keep it in check. I've had clients who got married for $10,000. I've had clients who got married for $200,000. And both had very beautiful weddings—the most important thing is making sure the day reflects the love they feel.

No budget is too small. But some budgets are too small for the kind of wedding the clients have in their heads. If they're open to different options, different venues, a different setup on the day of the wedding, then everything is possible. It's very common now for people to show me pictures they found online of wedding décor and insist this is exactly what they want. I tell them up front that replicating the photo is probably more expensive than they imagine. They may be showing me centrepieces that will cost thousands of dollars each. Flowers in Newfoundland are often air shipped from all over the world. A bunch of peonies in Toronto may cost $12 a bunch. Here they cost $28 a stem! It's my job to find alternatives, to come up with the same general look and feel as the Pinterest board of their dreams, but also making it fit within the budget.

There's almost nothing I won't do to make sure my clients have great wedding experiences. I've had brides who don't have close friends here, so I'll go dress shopping with them. I book hotels for guests coming from out of town and suggest touring activities. I can even offer advice on sensitive situations. For example, sometimes a close family member may have passed away just before the wedding. It can be very emotional dealing with that. I work with the couple to try to honour the memory of their loved one, while still celebrating their marriage. It's not unusual for the parents of the bride or groom to be divorced. The couple will come to me and ask, "Do we sit them at the same table? Or should we put them at separate tables? But then can we make sure that the tables are the exact same distance away from the head table so that they will feel like they're equally important?"

On the big day, I want everyone to be able to relax and enjoy themselves. The bride and groom, of course, but also their parents and families. They don't even have to know about the fires I'm putting out. At one wedding, the DJ thought the wedding was on Saturday, but it was on Friday. I had to find another DJ about an hour before the reception started. Another time, the person delivering the cake had a car accident on her way to the wedding. She was okay, but the cake was ruined. It was quite a scramble to get another cake at the eleventh hour.

It's my job to discreetly deal with any situation that arises. At a wedding a few years ago, a couple's uncle had a few too many at an open-bar cocktail hour, and by the time dinner was served, he couldn't sit up straight in his chair. Then he started to heckle the emcee and people who were making speeches. I made up some excuse that I needed him to help with something in the bar area and got him out of there. I ended up just standing at the bar talking to him for an hour and a half to keep him entertained while they finished speeches and the dinner.

Of course, I should probably admit there are hitches. There are bad speeches at many weddings, and we all grin and bear it. I try to encourage people to keep it short, but things happen. Sometimes someone will have a very nice three-minute speech prepared, but they'll ad lib a joke and a few people will laugh. That will inspire another joke, and before you know it, we're off the rails. But we recover pretty quickly. Almost always, things work, even with hurricanes.

After more than a decade planning weddings, I am still just as obsessed with love stories as when I started. There's a magic that happens at weddings when I see the couple in their love bubble. It's infectious. My favourite moments are the glimpses I see between the scheduled events of the day, like the kiss, the bouquet toss, the speeches. It's when no one is looking, but I see the couple absorbed in each other and the wonder of the day. It's not showy. It's pure, unvarnished love. Everything else falls away—all the details, the stresses, the expectations, even the budget. Those are the moments that I work for. Because everyone deserves to celebrate their love and create the best memories.

*Stories transport us to new worlds, and so often bringing
those stories to life are actors, whose job it is to make us forget
about our realities for the space of an hour or two and immerse
ourselves in a different time and place, where we might learn
something new. One such actor is Mike Nadajewski, who has
spent most of his career playing featured roles at Canada's
major theatre festivals, particularly Stratford and Shaw.*

◆

# THE ACTOR
## Mike Nadajewski

It was terrifying. I was acting in a Sherlock Holmes mystery at
the Shaw Festival. Suddenly, I couldn't remember my next line. I
watched the blood drain from the face of the actor I was speaking to
as she realized I had gone completely blank. Usually, I'm able to finesse
a momentary block. I can kind of stumble over something, maybe just
say something else. This was one of the few times I went completely
blank. I just lost the thread.

There was an excruciatingly long pause, until finally she just decided it was time to move on.

It was mortifying. To this day, I still can't believe it happened. But these moments happen as a stage actor, and the show must always go on.

Over the course of my career, I've memorized a lot of lines, but I still remember every line from my high school production of *Cabaret* more than twenty-five years ago. Because it was the show that changed my life.

It was my first year of high school. I was just looking to find friends and something to do, and I thought I would audition for the school play and see if I could make it into the ensemble. Four amazing teachers saw something in me and gave me the part of the emcee, the role made famous by Joel Grey in the movie, and set me on a career path that I would never have had if not for those four brilliant teachers. It chokes me up to talk about it—the fundamental importance of teachers who really see their students and believe in them.

That *Cabaret* experience was a eureka moment for me. I obviously knew there was theatre in Toronto. *Phantom of the Opera*. *Cats*. But it had never occurred to me that the actors in those shows probably started just like this. In a high school play. The notion that I could be like them was thrilling.

I started looking outside of school to keep acting. I did some community theatre, and one of the people there put me in touch with an agent. When I finished high school, he encouraged me not to go to university right away. And surprisingly, my teachers and parents were okay with that. They all said, "Give it a year and see what happens."

It was a major decision. I had a choice between several universities or striking out on my own. I was worried that if I continued with school, I'd lose my gumption. When you're young, you feel you can do anything, and I seemed to learn best by being thrown into the deep end of the pool and forced to swim.

I deferred university and gave show business one year. I took acting classes and went to auditions everywhere I could. Auditions aren't usually the cattle calls you sometimes see in movies or on TV. When you walk into the room, the people running things want you to be the right person, they really do. They want you to do well, and they want you to succeed. That's a palpable thing you can feel.

Still, I don't think any actor likes auditions, and I'm no different. But no actor turns down an audition because it's an opportunity, a chance to show yourself in a way that maybe the people on the other side of the table haven't seen before. You don't want to be typecast and miss out on roles you think you can do but no one else thinks you're even interested in. An audition can be an opportunity to show that you have range and that you can do something different. That's how you build a body of work.

When I wasn't going to auditions, I was working at Moores, the suit store, in the back as a stockboy, with a guy who didn't even know my name. He just kept calling me Johnny.

Six months went by, and I was getting nowhere in the way of acting. "Fine," I thought. "I'll be going to school in six months, and at least I tried."

Then I got my first show, and that show led to the next show, and work just beget work, and I began to meet people and network, and that's how my career was born. All these years later, I guess you could call me an established actor, but in this line of work, your next show is never guaranteed, and there is no steady ascension to the top where you only play the lead. While there are some theatre organizations where I don't have to audition, there are some that I do. At Stratford, they pretty well make everyone audition. The actors have to fit into several shows, so sometimes I have to audition for just one show, and then, because other directors may know me, they can say, "Yeah, he would fit here and here." Sometimes I get the lead, sometimes I'm in a supporting role, and sometimes I'm in the ensemble. In terms of survival, being a working actor is being a successful actor.

Which is why I approached acting as a job and continued to diversify my portfolio of skills, to broaden my horizons, sharpen my toolkit. When I was first getting roles, it was mostly in musical theatre, so I took classes at the Birmingham Conservatory at the Stratford Festival under the leadership of Martha Henry to gain more experience with Shakespeare, who I found intimidating then, but who I now love.

Once you get a role, it's your job, and you have to learn it. That

*Performing* Cabaret *at the Royal Manitoba Theatre Centre twenty-two years after that first high school performance that changed my life. I'm in the very middle.*

means memorizing lines, which can be grueling. There's no secret formula for doing it. It's just repetition, repetition, repetition. I sit on my couch, read a line, say it out loud, then I say it again. I get a little further, then I go back. Over and over. I find that sleep is huge. That's when the lines move from short-term to longer-term memory. If I can get a good chunk of memorizing time before I go to bed, then as soon as I wake up, I go over it again, and it's suddenly there.

It helps to read the play a couple of times as well, just to connect the dots. If it's a well-written play, you should be able to follow the line of thinking, and that helps quite a bit.

There was a season at Stratford that I found out rather late that I was the understudy for the role of Hamlet. It's one of the largest parts in the English language. I spent ten arduous weeks trying to cram it into my brain. I even calculated that I had to learn nineteen lines a day. This was all on the off chance that I'd be needed if the real Hamlet got sick and had to miss a show. At the same time, I was rehearsing my own shows.

Of course, knowing your lines in a play isn't enough. The magic is rattling off something like Oscar Wilde's brilliance ("Relations are simply a tedious pack of people who haven't got the remotest knowledge of how to live, nor the smallest instinct about when to die.") as if I just thought of it. If you think too much about how tough all that is, you can spook yourself.

One way that theatre is different from film and television is that it's live, every time. Which means I might be performing the same role seven or eight times a week for several months. When I'm doing the same thing over and over again, I can't let it get monotonous. The audience can never feel that they're watching just another Wednesday matinee. They should feel something that's really special, that what's happening is just for them.

The truth is that sometimes I'm really up for a show and sometimes I'm just not. Maybe I'm tired because I had a bad sleep. Maybe my son was up all night. Actors are real people with real lives. Then we have to come to work and act in a play. I'm not always able to count on my inner spark to animate my performance, but I can rely on my training and all the practicing I've done to make the audience believe that I am doing it for the first time, just for them. That's my job.

What's not my job is worrying about the critics. I figured out years ago that what critics write about me is none of my business. Good or bad, a review has the potential to affect my performance. If I get a bad review, well, no one likes reading anything negative about themselves; there is enough rejection in this business without having to read it in print! Depending on how confident I feel in the work, a critic's negative response could plant a seed of doubt in what the director and I have set, making it a challenge to act out the entire run of the play, which could be several months.

If I get a good review, if someone says I'm brilliant and mentions a particular moment when I'm especially brilliant, then when I'm doing the show, I start thinking, "Oh, here comes that great moment." Which isn't helpful. It has nothing to do with my job, which is to act in this play and to care only about how well this scene is being received right now by the audience in front of me. It's the healthiest, the only way, I think, to survive.

I'm happy to have survived this long. I love what I do, though it isn't always easy, and I sometimes struggle with parts of it, like being away from my family so much, fatigue, anxiety, and vocal stress. As I get older, it gets harder to protect my voice. Alcohol dries out my voice, so

I don't drink anymore. I can't even finish a beer because the negative effect is so dramatic. I lose some of my range. I also have a contraption that lets me inhale steam, which I use most nights because I want to be able to sing without worrying that the notes are going to fall away, or my voice will break. The notes are either there or they're not; there's really nothing in between.

Throughout my career, but especially during the COVID pandemic, I have had heart-to-heart talks with my wife about whether it's time to make a shift, to look for another line of work. We always conclude that I'm an actor, and I would miss doing something that makes me feel good and connects me with people. I realize that might be selfish. I know that when the Zombie Apocalypse comes, no one is going to be scrambling to save the Shakespearean actors. But I also know that to have a healthy, functioning, empathetic, and generous society, you need the arts. That's where I fit in in this world.

*Who doesn't like a zoo? For generations, people, kids especially, have been transported to worlds far and wide by going to the local zoo. It's a day they'll never forget, a day they'll tell their kids about. The Edmonton Valley Zoo attracts more than 12 million visitors every year. That's right, 12 million. Making it all work are people like Trevor Hickey, who has been one of its zookeepers for fifteen years.*

◆

# THE ZOOKEEPER
## Trevor Hickey

One of my greatest days as a zookeeper was the day I got a camel to step onto a scale. While that might not sound like a big deal to many people, it was for us at the Edmonton Valley Zoo.

Before that, we hadn't been able to weigh our camel because we didn't have a scale that was big enough. Then when we got one, the camel was afraid. They're prey animals, and so they take careful note of changes in their environment. They are wary of new things because it may mean a predator is getting ready to pounce. So, I had to create trust between me and that animal. The moment when he overcame his fear of stepping on that big scary white square that makes noise and is slippery and just stood there was incredible. It showed me that the bond we had was very strong.

And that's the case for most animals and their zookeepers. Many of the animals at Edmonton Valley Zoo I know from the time they're born to the time they die. Unfortunately, animals don't live as long as people, so I've seen quite a few animals pass away after they've lived very full lives, but it's always difficult. As a zookeeper, I have a professional responsibility to make sure that they are living the best lives they can, and while I know they're not pets or just here at the zoo for me, it's impossible to care *for* an animal without caring *about* the animal.

One of our arctic wolves, Shilah, is about fifteen years old now, which is very old for a wolf. I've known her for her entire life, worked with her closely, spent a lot of time with her, but now she's nearing the end of her life. We don't expect her to live another full year, but we don't know how she'll go. The best case is that she has a heart attack in her sleep. She's also showing some signs of degeneration of the nerves in her back. She's not in a lot of pain, but she walks kind of funny. If she reaches a point where she's not able to walk anymore, then we would likely have to euthanize her. I'd have to put a leash and a muzzle on her so the vet could do what has to be done without getting bit. It's my duty to her as a zookeeper.

Thankfully, the job isn't so emotionally draining most of the time. In fact, it's highly rewarding, and it keeps me very busy. We are one of twenty-five accredited zoos and aquariums in Canada, and we have more than 350 animals. I feed and clean up after all of them. I toss hay bales and chop fruits and vegetables. I get rats for the snakes and feed meatballs to the tigers. Every animal gets what it specifically requires.

*Me with Shilah, the wolf.*

They all need water, but not the same water. For example, frogs don't really drink water; they absorb it through their skin. You can't just give a frog tap water or it's going to die.

But sometimes, an animal needs more than everyday food and water. We had to hand raise a baby camel because its mother didn't want anything to do with it. When she had a second baby, she showed positive signs of accepting it, but the baby just couldn't latch; it wouldn't find the udder. If this happened in the wild, the mother might just leave that animal, and a lion would come eat it, but this isn't the wild. We can take the animal and give it a milk replacer, and we can eventually reintroduce it to its herd, and so within a year it will be back to being a normal camel.

Teaching the animals veterinary behaviours is also a big part of my job. We have a harbour seal who suffers from seizures. We're not sure why she has them, but we've trained her to allow blood to be drawn from a vein in her tail. She'll sit very still and let us put the needle in. Then we can send the blood away for testing so that we know her medication is doing what it's supposed to do. We've also trained animals to take medications that might taste yucky. They open their mouth so we can squirt it in.

As a zookeeper, I also provide the animals with opportunities to express their natural behaviour. We work with wild exotic animals, and some of them only exhibit very specific behaviours when they're faced with certain stimuli, so we try to replicate this in captivity. Take our Goeldi's monkeys. They eat a lot of tree sap, which means in the wild they have to bite on a certain branch to get the sap out. There's not a lot of tree sap available commercially for us to give them, but we squish some fruit into a rough log, and that way the monkeys can get it out the way they would in the wild.

Another example is our otters. They like to dive down to the bottom of the river to get clams. We buy clams for them, but they often float to the surface. So I built a little device that allows us to put the clams inside a little container and sink it to the bottom of the water. The otters dive down, manipulate the container, open it up, and then they can get their clams. Elephants like to reach for their food, push stuff over, break branches, strip bark off trees. If we just give them piles of hay on the floor, it isn't very enticing. So we put hay into nets, so the elephants have to reach up and pull. We also provide the elephants with whole trees so they can pull at the leaves and branches, expressing natural behaviours.

I like providing social companionship to the animals. I spend so much time building relationships and interacting with them, I think they get to know me. They don't know I'm Trevor Hickey, but a lot of them recognize that I'm a member of their care team, and that I wear a blue shirt and khaki pants and I have keys that jingle when I walk. In fact, here's a tip for anyone visiting a zoo. Wear clothes with the same colour scheme as the zookeepers' uniform and jingle some keys. Chances are, more animals will come over to check you out.

I'm comfortable with the animals, but I never forget they are wild animals who will sometimes behave in ways we don't expect. It can be exciting when an animal surprises us with different behaviours. But we don't want nasty surprises, and we are careful to minimize risk.

For example, we can't go in with our tigers. The potential for large carnivores to kill us is very high. If you're hand-rearing a tiger cub because the mother has rejected it, that's fine. But once they're three months old, they aren't nursing anymore, so we don't share space with them. I also don't go in with our male camel. He weighs 750 kg, and if he perceives me as a threat to his power over female camels, he might trample me. I can go in with the females because they aren't territorial. I don't go in with the male zebra, not because he's exceptionally dangerous but because he's so focused on getting to his females, he might not be sure to avoid knocking me over when he's running to them.

As a zookeeper, I care about our animals, but sometimes, I've wondered whether working at a zoo is the right thing. It isn't a natural place. We take animals from all over the world and put them on a forty-eight-hectare plot of land in Edmonton. There's nothing natural about that. But then I remind myself that the zoo isn't just here for people to look at animals. It's here to conserve wildlife.

For example, the California condor would not exist today if it weren't for the work of the San Diego Zoo. There are dozens of bird and mammal species that would likely be extinct if it weren't for zoos, nor would the wild Mongolian horse (Przewalski's horses) exist. That animal went extinct in the wild in the 1960s, but thanks to zoos, there's now a viable population back in its native area, and more than a hundred reintroduction programs are going on.

At our zoo, we raise these animals to be ambassadors for their wild counterparts. Nearly 99 percent of the animals we have were born in captivity. We have very few that were caught in the wild, and those were probably injured and deemed non-releasable. If they weren't zoo animals, they wouldn't be wild animals, they'd be dead animals.

A huge part of our work is education, to get people to understand the terrible stuff that we've done to this world and how it's impacting animals. If we want people to care about something, we need to create an emotional connection, and we can do that with animals a lot easier than we can plants. When people can look into an animal's eyes and see a little bit of themselves reflected, then maybe they will make some changes in their lives so that animals can live in the wild the way they are supposed to.

*Ready for a stunning statistic? There are more than 7,000 languages spoken on our planet today. No one can speak or understand them all, but luckily, we have people who speak and understand more than one, and they help bridge the communication gap between us. Like Dagmar Rathjen, who has been working for the government of Canada as an interpreter for more than thirty years.*

---

# THE INTERPRETER
## Dagmar Rathjen

Most Canadians may think of me as a translator, but that is not what I am. Translation is written. Interpretation is verbal. To simultaneously interpret is to listen, decode (that is, figure out the meaning of what a person is saying), and speak—all at the same time. A translator writes down words that remain forever, so a translation must be precise. Interpretation means extracting meaning from speech in real time and to convey this meaning as faithfully as possible—under the circumstances—into another language.

I learned three languages from a very young age. My parents were born in Germany, and German is my mother tongue. I went to school in French in Quebec from elementary through high school and cégep, and my university studies were also in French. English? Well, I learned that by osmosis. I studied translation at the University of Ottawa, but because of my personality (which is outgoing, whereas translation is a solitary occupation), my professors nudged me towards interpretation. So I took a couple of interpretation classes, and though I graduated with good marks, in my heart of hearts I felt this profession would be too daunting for me. Besides, I was only in my early twenties and wanted to see more of the world before settling into a job. So, I worked as a tour director and led bus tours, mostly for Germans, across Canada. In retrospect, I realize this was a good training ground for a career as an interpreter. I had to think quickly on my feet, remain calm at all times, and solve any problems that unexpectedly came up. Still, I knew I did not want to work in tourism for the rest of my life, so after three years, armed with more emotional and intellectual maturity, I finally decided to become a simultaneous interpreter.

I showed up at the courthouse in Montreal, introduced myself, and asked if they were looking to hire court interpreters. The man in charge told me to shadow the senior interpreters for as long as I thought necessary to hone my skills, and then he would give me an assignment. That was it? Just study and work on my own until I felt ready? No problem. And this trait, the ability to buckle down and self-teach, is one all interpreters share. So for three weeks, I followed the senior interpreters around, took notes, learned the jargon of the court, and at the end, I was hired.

But even then, I knew my goal was to work on Parliament Hill with some of the best interpreters in the world. At the time, I had a friend who was an interpreter in Ottawa, and I asked her to send me the reports of the auditor general of Canada. These were physical copies—there were no computers back then—and during my down-time in court, I read those reports and learned the vocabulary of government.

When positions opened in Ottawa, I applied. I passed all the aptitude tests, was hired, and then went through another three months of training. Today, I have more than thirty years of experience under my belt, and I still get a thrill when I'm on Parliament Hill and working in that beautiful environment—the marble floors, the wood, the sculptures, the paintings. And I still get the same intellectual high from the work, especially after a meeting when I know I did a good job.

Everything the government does has to be conducted in both official languages, so Canadians probably hear us most often when

*In the English interpretation booth at the House of Commons.*

we work in the House of Commons. But there is so much more to it than that. Interpreters work at caucus meetings for political parties, at cabinet meetings and retreats, at news conferences and committee meetings, at federal marketing boards, and so on. We also travel with official delegations and parliamentary committees. Everywhere, interpreters are the proverbial fly on the wall.

Like all parliamentary interpreters, I am completely apolitical. Interpreters must be perceived as neutral and objective. We have top-secret security clearance. We are privileged observers, sometimes to important moments of history, but we can never speak about them— and we never do. As soon as we leave a closed meeting, it's over and forgotten.

As a parliamentary interpreter, I also do what is called "elbow interpreting" or "whisper interpreting." For example, a colleague and I travelled to Washington a few times with the international trade committee. There were a couple of Bloc Québécois members on the committee, and we met a congressman in his office. We sat behind our clients, at their elbow, and whispered a French interpretation of what the congressman was saying. Then we interpreted from French to English when the member responded. We had to train the members because the back-and-forth in the conversation had to flow, and if a member went on for too long, this flow would be interrupted. We might gently tap a member's arm to remind him to pause. Then we would interpret the intervention, after which they would continue, and so on.

In the House and Senate, interpreters are a little removed from their clients because we work in booths which blend into the surroundings. I am a people person, so I love working closely with my clients and getting to know them as more than disembodied voices. However, most often, interpreters work in the shadows. We do not want to be seen, only heard.

In a manner of speaking, we live inside people's heads. And since everybody has a different worldview and different thoughts and experiences, we need to know a little about everything. An interpreter is not just someone who is good with languages. We have curious and quick minds, and we need constant intellectual stimulation. We feed off new experiences because that is how our brains are wired. It is both a blessing and a curse. We can be very restless.

This is a profession most people enter in their late twenties or early thirties because, as alluded to above, being an interpreter requires a certain degree of life experience, as well as a certain degree of intellectual and emotional maturity.

For myself and many of my colleagues, the path to interpretation was not linear. Some were lawyers, others worked in communications. We have many creative types—musicians and singers. Many were professional translators before making the leap into interpretation. We all have varied life experiences, and these many reference points mean we have more resources to draw upon in the course of our work. Because any topic can come up at any time.

As for rendering the message, or the meaning, we do the best we can under the circumstances. Those three words, *under the circumstances*, are key. If a speaker is reading a speech at the speed of light, if the sound quality is poor (which can be due to countless reasons), if there are loud background noises, if the sound cuts in and out, if there is static on the line, if a speaker mumbles in his beard, if another has a speech impediment or a heavy accent, if people tap into their microphones, or if there is feedback because an earpiece is placed too closely to the mic, we do the best we humanly can in the working conditions at hand.

Even in the best of circumstances, we cannot afford to be perfectionists. We cannot get hung up on finding that perfect idiomatic expression every time, because we risk getting stuck and missing what the speaker is saying next. So, we simply render the meaning of what was just said and move on. Besides, there are many ways of rendering an idea. It doesn't matter what words you use. As long as you get the meaning across in proper English (or French, or whatever your target language is) and your interpretation flows, and your clients understand the meaning of what a speaker is saying, then you've done your job.

At a committee meeting years ago, I was interpreting from French into English when a member from Quebec said, "Si c'est pas cassé, répare-le pas." That is a word-for-word translation of "if it ain't broke, don't fix it," which is what I said in my interpretation. I was worried that the expression was too familiar, but the English-speaking members understood and ran with it. Another time, I was interpreting the former leader of the NDP, Jack Layton, at a news conference where he was talking about Canadians living in rural and urban areas. He was speaking very fast, so I said, "country folk and city folk," which, again, is not quite the register we aim for in parliament, and this made me anxious. However, the following day, *The Globe and Mail* quoted me exactly, which gave me no end of relief because my words had been validated by Canada's national newspaper. These are the things we interpreters worry about! No one but an interpreter would have batted an eye.

Every interpreter has their own style. Some do not convey much emotion, preferring to speak in a neutral voice. I am naturally more expressive and try to reflect the personality of the speaker through intonation and the use of pauses, and by putting a bit of colour into my voice (where appropriate, of course).

Then there is a speaker's speaking style. Of course, it varies from one person to the next. Some people are logical thinkers, and they are generally easier to interpret. Some do not speak in full sentences, some go off on tangents from which they never return, some do not understand punctuation marks and speak in a stream of consciousness, others breathe in all the wrong places, and so on. This makes our jobs more challenging, but also more interesting! We are always asking ourselves at the back of our minds "What is he (or she) *saying*?" At all times, however, an interpreter's delivery must sound credible, as we cannot lose the confidence of those who are listening to us. If we do not understand something or did not properly hear something, we do not let on, and carry on.

Often, the most difficult things to interpret are poems—written by members themselves or quoted from a work—or quotes from the Bible or some other authoritative source. If we receive advance notice, it can be a fun challenge to translate such a thing in advance. Sometimes, however, it is just not possible to interpret this type of thing cold. A few years ago, I was interpreting at a brief news conference between the Israeli and Canadian prime ministers. I had prepared as best I could, but none of the questions from the international press had anything to do with current world events. Rather, they were all about a political scandal happening in France. I was completely caught off guard but did my best on the fly. It was only after the event that I read up on the issue and could satisfy myself that my interpretation had been fine.

Another time, years ago, I was part of a joint House and Senate committee that was studying the use of illicit drugs. We travelled to a few European countries, including Germany. In Düsseldorf, we were all sitting around a big table. Our German hosts did not speak English or French. I am not accredited for German, but they needed me, and so I worked in three languages. I recall a Reform Party MP whose eyes got wider and wider as I hopped around from English to French to German. After the meeting, he said, "Wow, Dagmar, that was something." It was a special moment for me because I knew I was making a difference on a personal level, helping people understand each other.

I cannot pretend that every day is quite so rewarding. Sometimes I find myself at a meeting, listening to the same arguments and debates I'd heard years or decades before. But that is the exception. And while it is a privilege to work on Parliament Hill, simultaneous interpretation can be draining. We generally work in teams of three, each of us going for about twenty minutes before our brain needs a rest. It's akin to running a sprint, which you cannot do over a marathon distance. Your brain is a muscle which needs to rest and recover before resuming the race. At the end of a long day, most interpreters cannot handle any kind of stimuli—television, radio, kids, or any other type of interaction. We need to completely disconnect for a while and recharge our mental batteries.

Yet it is hard for me to turn off my interpreting brain completely. If I'm at a party and find myself in a boring conversation, I start asking myself, "How would I say that in French (or in a language other than the one the person across from me is speaking)?" If I'm in my car listening to Radio-Canada or the CBC, I will sometimes interpret out loud in English or French, just to keep my mind active.

In short, interpreters have brains which are wired in a unique way that lets us do the job we all love so much. It is incredibly gratifying to help people communicate across the linguistic divide.

*Malls are often the hubs of communities, the modern version of a market square. Not only are they important places of commerce that help make Canada work, but they're places for people to gather. Peter Havens is a self-proclaimed mall rat who, as the general manager of the fourteenth-largest mall in Canada, ensures everything is running smoothly.*

◆

# THE MALL MANAGER
## Peter Havens

I hate shopping. I know that's odd for a guy who works as the general manager of CF Polo Park, the biggest mall in Winnipeg. For most of my life, I would do anything to avoid shopping or going to a shopping mall. But that attitude helped me when I started in this industry. I thought that if I could figure out how to turn a mall into a place even I would like to shop, then it would be great for everyone. That's been a never-ending quest. When I go on vacations now, I take time to visit shopping centres to see if I can learn something new, to see if they're doing something interesting that I can bring home.

CF Polo Park is a two-level mall with more than 100,000 square metres of retail space and 179 stores, and over 10 million people visit it in a year. As the general manager, I want to be invisible, especially from the customer's point of view. They're at the mall to shop; they don't need to be thinking about the person who is making sure the place is running smoothly—they just want it to do so. That's true of all shoppers, no matter if they're at the mall on a mission or there to browse.

Mission shoppers want to get in and get out as quickly and efficiently as possible. Our wayfinding (use of signs and design to help people navigate spaces) has to be good for that person. If it's a man who needs to buy a shirt from a specific store, he can use our app to tell him where the store is, and even which entrance to park at. He can accomplish his shirt-buying mission just like that, quickly and efficiently.

If he needs a shirt but doesn't know exactly what kind of shirt, his experience is a little different. He may stop at Guest Services and say, "I'm looking for a shirt. Any suggestions?" To my surprise, this happens a lot. When I started in the retail business, I thought people asked Guest Services where to find a particular store or brand. Our staff enjoys suggesting a few stores the shopper may go to and find the shirt they want.

Then there are those who use the mall as a destination, with no particular shopping goal. This person may do some browsing in several stores. Maybe they get a coffee at Tim Hortons or Starbucks, sit down, and scroll through their phone. They don't feel rushed, and I don't want them to feel rushed. In fact, there are many people who come to the mall and never shop. Some older folks come to sit around in the food court and chitchat. It's a social gathering spot akin to an old town square. They're not causing any problems, so I have no issues with that.

I also have no issues with young people who use the mall to hang out. I see parents drop off their teenagers who meet up with half a dozen friends and just walk around. Maybe they buy drinks or a snack, but they're not really shopping. They're just here to see and be seen. It adds to traffic in the mall, and that adds vibrancy to the place. And teenagers are the future. If they get comfortable here now, that should make them happy to come back when they're ready to shop as adults.

No matter what kind of shopper, or non-shopper, walks through our doors, I want them to feel safe. We have security patrols, and they're very visible. We also have cameras throughout the mall, and we watch the output from a control room for things that are out of place. The other day, we had a minor fender bender in the parking lot that created congestion, so our dispatcher got on the radio to the exterior patrol to go over and get them to move aside. We also watch for medical emergencies, or a child who might be wandering alone. We don't get a lot of lost children, but it happens often enough for us to have a special code on our radio so we can mobilize quickly to find the child. Our goal is to find the lost one within ninety seconds of getting a report. As a parent, I know I would want help fast, so it's something we take seriously.

Shoplifting goes on, of course. While every store is responsible for its own internal security, we work with them to reduce theft. But I would never want a security officer running down somebody who's stealing something. That's a recipe for escalation into a stabbing, a shooting, or a pepper spraying.

A major part of my job is keeping the storeowners happy. They are the tenants, and I am the landlord. I make it a point to walk around the mall every day and stop to talk to them. Sometimes I'm engaged with one of them for an hour, and I don't begrudge that hour because it builds a relationship. That comes in handy when problems arise down the road. If I'm dealing with someone on a regular basis, it makes it easier to work together to find solutions. I don't just want to say no when they ask for something. Though there are times they ask me for the impossible.

A tenant might complain that the road outside their storefront is bumpy, or it has a pothole. I can't control that. It's city property. I can call the city and ask that it be repaired, but that's all I can do. A few years ago, there was a huge City of Winnipeg construction project on the west side of the mall that messed up traffic and caused delays for people entering our property. Some tenants asked me, "How could you let this happen?" Well, what the city does is completely beyond my control.

I do better when the complaint is about something I can influence, such as the store being too hot or too cold. I can take that to one of our contractors and see if there's anything to be done.

I listen to tenant suggestions for improving the mall, and we try to take what they say into consideration when we invest in capital projects, such as upgrading our closed-circuit cameras, repainting the upper level of the mall, repaving part of our parking lot, and doing maintenance as well. I love my job because I get my fingers into things I'd never have a chance to touch otherwise. I've learned about different kinds of concrete, for example, and how to choose which one is best for a given circumstance. I like to think of myself as a connector, picking up a little bit of information from here, and then connecting it to something over there. It gives me a lot of satisfaction.

Christmas is a very important time because so much business happens. Those six weeks can make or break an entire year for a lot of retailers. A typical store may do half their yearly business around the holiday, so I'll do everything I can to make those weeks count. Especially since we were closed for two Christmases because of COVID.

That was an eerie time. When I walked through the empty mall, I realized how much I love and thrive off the vibrancy of a busy shopping season. Before Christmas, there's an energy, a buzz that's hard to explain unless you're physically feeling it. I didn't know how much I missed that until I didn't have it.

At Christmas, we welcome people to the mall who come only once

*At CF Polo Park being interviewed prior to*
*the COVID restrictions being lifted.*

a year. They're rediscovering the place, so we endeavour to make sure their experience is pleasant. We pay special attention to helping them get around, finding the stores they want, and reducing congestion in any way we can.

I tell my staff that if we can help create a good experience for the tenants, that will trickle down so that they're creating a good experience for the customers, who will stay here longer and spend more money. On the other hand, hurting shoppers, doing things they don't like, or even being indifferent to them, means they will respond with their feet and leave.

Going the extra mile for a shopper is never a bad idea. One of my favourite examples came from one of my security guards, a super-nice burly guy, who was just walking the mall when he noticed somebody who seemed to be struggling to find their way around. He went up to her and asked if he could help in any way. She said she was there to pay a bill but was visually impaired and was having trouble finding where she wanted to go. My guard said, "Just take my arm," and he guided her to her destination.

I wouldn't have known about this—the guard didn't say anything to me—but the woman called to say how much she appreciated one of my staff going above and beyond to help her. That was a great day for me. Thousands of people go through the shopping centre every day. Touching one or two in a positive and meaningful way counts for a lot.

I have the best retail job there is. I'm a paid mall rat.

*How many times have you heard someone say, "Small businesses are the backbone of the Canadian economy." You've heard it a lot because it's true. The 1.2 million small businesses together generate almost half of the GDP produced by the private sector and, collectively, are the country's largest employer, putting more than 8.4 million Canadians to work. Steve Rafael and his brother Elan are one of those small businesses.*

◆

# THE BAKERY OWNER
## Steve Rafael

I once worked more than one hundred days in a row. And if you think that's crazy, what's even crazier is that I was proud of it.

I was about thirty years old when I joined my older brothers and mom as an owner of Kiva's, a bakery and restaurant in Toronto, and I didn't know better.

Fifteen years later, I would never ever do that to myself. I hadn't learned how to delegate. I was the boss of people who were much older than me, often twice my age and more, but I thought I had to do everything. I was waking up at about four a.m., going weeks at a time without a day off. I didn't manage my time properly. These days, I get to the store at around six a.m., try to leave by four p.m., work only six days a week, and I plan for vacation time.

We have three locations, but all the baking is done at my store. So the morning begins by supervising the loading of our trucks with the food for the other stores. I make sure the drivers have everything because forgetting something means they have to make an extra trip later, or we have to Uber the forgotten things downtown.

The bakers have been in since about three a.m. The day before, they spent hours hand-rolling bagels and preparing breads and buns, cakes and cookies. We make about 2,000 bagels every day. After they're rolled, they're put into the fridge overnight to proof, which is when the dough undergoes its final rise. That makes a New York–style bagel. Montreal-style bagels are boiled in water and honey, then cooked in a wood-fired oven. And they're smaller.

Our bakers start their day by taking the bagels from the fridge, throwing them into the kettle to boil for a minute or two, then scooping them out, sprinkling on the seeds, and slamming them into the oven. The bagels are baked at a very high temperature, then we lower the temperature for the breads and buns. The cakes and cookies come after that.

It's hard to run a small business because there are so many different aspects to it. We don't just have a bakery. We have a restaurant. And there's catering too, not large events like weddings, but we make platters for smaller parties and gatherings—sandwiches and pastries. That has to be prepared and delivered too. So my brain is often pulled in three or four directions at once.

By nine a.m., the restaurant is full, and the rest of the day flies by as I seat customers and make sure things are running smoothly. If our servers are running around and seem anxious, I help out, taking menus and coffee to tables. As I refill coffees, I get the chance to walk by every table and see how the customers are doing.

My day is all movement. Circles and circles. From the restaurant to the bakery, back to the restaurant, and on it goes. I don't have an office. If I was in an office, I'd probably fall asleep in my chair. I'm on my feet most of the day. I even used to eat standing up, but now I try to sit down. I do stop circling from time to time to make phone calls (standing up). I have a list of things I have to do on the phone. There's a lot of ordering of materials, for example. Flour and yeast for the bakery. All the food for the restaurant—vegetables, cheese, eggs, coffee, juices, canned goods. And I'm always writing notes to myself because if I don't write down that we have to order sprinkles for the sprinkle cookies the instant I notice, I'll forget.

Many years ago, a customer pointed out to my mother that I was running around like a madman. He said to her, "Your son goes around and around. I don't think he knows what he's doing." She started laughing. "No, he knows what he's doing. The faster he runs, the more smoothly the business runs."

All the walking around does have a side benefit: I burn calories. Which is a good thing because I do taste everything in the store. I can't just open up in the morning and serve whatever comes out of the kitchen. I have to make sure everything tastes like it should. I'm quality control. I don't taste everything every day, of course, but I run through the marble cake and the babka, the cheese Danish and the rugelach over time. And I eat lots of broken cookies. The other day, a gingerbread cookie broke. I never eat gingerbread, as it's for kids. But

*Making my rounds with the coffee pot on a busy morning at Kiva's.*

I ate this cookie, and it was so delicious. In the restaurant, the cooks experiment with stuff all the time. Last week, one of them called me over to taste a salmon steak. It was so good, we put that on our menu as a daily special.

Nothing is more important to any business than the customer. I strive for 100 percent customer satisfaction every day. I want to make sure that every customer who comes in leaves happy. Because if they're not happy, they're not going to come back. That old expression about the customer always being right? Sometimes it's not true, but I have to pretend it's true when someone complains that a bagel is not fresh. I know with absolute certainty that in my store there is no such thing as a not-fresh bagel. Every one of them is baked that morning. What the customer may really be saying is that the bagel is over-baked. Of course, that's a matter of taste. Some customers prefer a bagel that's well done. Others like theirs lightly baked. Some like a lot of seeds, some just a few seeds. So, "not fresh" really means "It's not what I prefer." Which is fine. I can probably find a bagel more to their liking.

Once the lunch rush is over, I turn my attention to the next day. I look at the orders we have, give the bakers their notes for anything special. Two dozen bagels lightly done. One dozen twisters extra well done. I make them a daily production list of how many bagels, pastries, muffins, cookies, breads, and buns they need to bake. I base that on the season—winter is slower than summer—and on the day of the week—Monday through Thursday is kind of the same, then from Friday to Sunday, each day gets busier.

If everything works out, we make just enough. We don't want to run out of things. But we don't want to make too much either. Like I said, we don't sell anything but bagels and breads made that same day (except for a little we sell at half price and label "day olds"). We try not to throw away any food. The food bank comes and picks up leftovers almost every day. Lasagnas, eggplant, blintzes, you name it. When things are on their last day, I give it away. Instead of going to waste, delicious food is put to good use.

When my day ends at the store, I try not to take work home with me, but sometimes that's impossible. I may not have had time to finish writing up a large order, or I may not have called for all the food we have to get. Sometimes I have to complete the staff schedule.

I've been blessed with great staff. We have a really strong bakery team. The servers are excellent. And the busboys are the backbone of the business. They not only clean the tables, but they also do the dishwashing, they put away deliveries and organize everything, and they mop and sweep the floors at the end of the day. Good employees are so important. My worst days are when I'm understaffed. People call in to say they can't work because they're sick, or their baby is sick, or their car broke down. It's all legitimate and understandable, but those days are not fun for me.

When inflation started to rise very fast in 2022, we had to rethink our prices. It seemed like every week we'd get a notice that the price of flour or canola oil was going up. Then gasoline prices went up (remember, we have trucks making deliveries) and the cost of labour went up. We didn't want to raise our prices, but in the end, we did to keep Kiva's running because it's everything to us. It's not just a bakery, or just a restaurant, or just a place to make a living. I see my days as a symphony, a whirl and mixture of events, full of life.

*Canada works because its people do, and in many cases, that doesn't happen by accident. Headhunters place the right people in jobs across the country's many industries. Like Jennifer Ward, a partner at Odgers Berndtson in Calgary. For more than thirty years, she's recruited top executives, including CEOs, COOs, CFOs, presidents, and vice presidents, for major corporations, both public and private.*

---

# THE HEADHUNTER
## Jennifer Ward

Most of us know what it's like applying for a job. You submit a resume and write a cover letter that you hope will stand out from all the other resumes and cover letters. Recruiting, or headhunting, turns that on its head. A company enlists us to pitch them to potential employees.

In my early years, when someone called me a headhunter, it was usually said with disdain. But the term doesn't carry the same stigma anymore. Now, I'm quite comfortable being called a headhunter. The important thing to emphasize is that I'm looking for just the right head, and the hunt is carefully, painstakingly, calculated to accomplish that. I don't wing it. In fact, it's because the hunt is so rigorous that companies hire us in the first place. They know they can't do the search as thoroughly by themselves.

I work with a team of two or three others on every search, and at the beginning of the process, we spend a lot of time with our client, understanding very clearly what their business problem is and how they expect this new individual to solve that problem. That upfront work takes hours, sometimes weeks. It's vital to get everything on the table.

It sounds so basic, but the compensation the company has in mind can be the most involved part of the headhunting process. I once had a client who was fixed on a salary range for the position of chief financial officer. We went to market with the posting, and after several weeks we found that the most suitable candidates were way beyond the compensation range that the company wanted to pay. So we had another conversation, and the company agreed that they needed to offer more. That has a domino effect internally, of course, because if one salary goes up, everyone in the organization wants their salary to go up. But at least we've dealt with the initial salary problem before the process reaches the final stage. We don't want to find a great candidate, then have the company present an offer, and have the person say, "You're off your rocker. I'm not coming for that!" That shouldn't ever happen when I lead a search. And again, that's because of our upfront work.

When I'm looking to fill the position of CEO for a company, I want to spend time with as many of the board directors as I can to understand how each of them feels about the search they're about to undertake. There's a lot at stake for that company. What's important to them? What do they need to see in the candidates? It's critical that I get their input because if that board doesn't agree on what it's looking for, they're not going to agree on any of the candidates I bring them. If there's no consensus from the start, we're setting up ourselves and our client for failure.

I look for intangibles too. I once did a search for a major airline that needed an executive who had very specific experience within the airline sector, which they were able to define pretty clearly. But in asking about the culture of the airline and discovering what made it unique, I could tell that someone who had the specific experience required but at an airline with a different culture would not slip easily into this one.

Once I have a clear picture of the kind of person I need to find, the next step is to find out where that person *is*, specifically *where* they're working now. It could be a company right around the corner, or maybe elsewhere in Canada, or it could be in another country entirely. We create a map, or a list of companies who employ the kind of person we're looking for, then we reach out to individuals at those businesses. Depending on the role and depending on how specific it is, we often approach about 100 people or more.

At the executive level, effective leaders are contacted all the time by headhunters, possibly every week. It's rare to get an executive on the phone without going through layers of gatekeepers, so usually we focus on writing the perfect email pitch to catch their attention. We really work on this. We're trying for a concise pitch that makes the prospective candidate sit back and say, "I get these all the time, but this one's really interesting." For every 100 feelers we cast out to our candidate universe, we might get fifteen bites.

Reeling them in is kind of tricky.

We've let them know how highly we think of them and indicated they might be the perfect person for this new opportunity, which is all true, but they're not the only person we've pitched. So once we have their interest, we have to delicately tell them that they're competing with other people—and not just any people, people just as impressive as them.

That competition begins with a screening process, usually two one-hour interviews. Someone from my team will have conversations with the prospective hires, ask them a few questions to ensure they're interested in the job and that they tick enough boxes. Right experience. Right temperament. And then there's DEI—Diversity, Equity, and Inclusion—which has become an important part of our work. The majority of our clients tell us they would like candidates who represent the diversity of our society. They might instruct us to bring them a short list that is 50 percent not white male. As a headhunter, I'd be the first to say that a perfect resume and list of credentials doesn't mean the candidate is a perfect fit for the role—it's the collective experience that they bring to the table that makes them a good fit, and we put a lot of time and effort into making sure our clients consider that.

In any case, once my colleagues are done with the preliminary vetting, it's my turn for a deep dive with each candidate. I sit with them for at least an hour, often much longer, for what I think of as the art of the search. Everything appears to be good, but are they? First, I look at motivation. Why would they leave the company they're at now? There has to be some sort of wound. What itch isn't being scratched in their current role?

One of the first things I learned in this business is that if the candidate's motivation is just to earn more money, we should back away because the candidate is likely to get the money anywhere. If I approach a candidate and she tells me, "I need to make another $30,000," I know

*A typical day on the hunt.*

that's doable. But when she goes to resign, her current employer may offer that same amount to get her to stay. In those cases, the candidate will frequently stay where they're at, and then I've wasted my client's time and my own time. So the wound I'm looking for is rarely about money.

It's more about personal satisfaction. Nowadays, many people who have a history of making six figures a year are willing to work for less if they can do something they consider more meaningful. There's a good amount of people in Alberta now, for instance, who would like to transition away from oil and gas and leverage the experience they've gained in the industry to apply it towards clean technology or energy transition. They know full well that they likely won't have a big salary and perks. But they'll get out of bed in the morning and feel good about going to work. That's the itch I'm looking for: people who are motivated by opportunity, who are motivated by the impact they can make in an organization.

Another topic I tackle right at the outset of the search is family. A candidate can be miserable in their current role, but it's a big decision to disrupt their family with a career move, potentially in another city, that's not guaranteed to work out. We vet this up front. Are they willing to uproot their family for this opportunity? Do they have buy-in from their family? The last thing we want is to go so far down the hiring path to the point that the client has met the candidate and is preparing an offer, only to have the candidate say they haven't really discussed it yet with their family. While it's a good thing for people to care about their families, they can make or break a deal. Which is why in our business we call families "deal killers," especially if the job requires the candidate to relocate.

And even still, a placement can go sideways. The candidate I found for the executive position at that major airline was from a faraway part of the world, and he had pre-teen kids and a spouse, who were all excited to move to Canada. It seemed like a grand adventure. They arrived here in November of 2019, experienced a terribly harsh winter, and then in March, the pandemic hit. The kids were never able to settle in at school and make friends. Things went badly for that poor family, and even though none of it was my fault, my heart ached for them. That's the hardest part of the job for me—the toll that choices can have on people and their families. It doesn't happen that way very often, but when it does, it hurts.

I talk to my client frequently throughout the process so that when I'm satisfied that I've found a short list of genuine candidates, it doesn't come as a surprise. At that point, they've seen all the resumes and we've talked about their strengths and weaknesses along the way, and they can feel confident that the person they're looking for is on that list.

A long time ago, I was told, "When you interact with people in this industry, you can't help them all. Maybe you can't even help most of them. But what you can do is make sure they feel better for having interacted with you." That's advice I try to live by. When I place somebody in a role, I've spent so much time with them, they often become a friend. I feel a connection to them and a responsibility. There's one man I've placed four times over the thirty years I've been headhunting. The first time, he was fresh out of MBA school, and now he's a CEO. That doesn't happen with every person I recruit, but I feel lucky when it does because it means I'm helping people—the companies and the employees—find the perfect fit. That's what I try to do each and every time I go out on a search.

*Home is where the heart is, but when we travel—whether it's for work or pleasure—hotels become our temporary home, and a good experience is often just as much about the hotel as it is about the people in the hospitality industry who make us feel like we are at home. People like Eugénie Jason, who is the general manager of Muir, Halifax's luxury hotel, which in 2023 was ranked ninth in the world by* AFAR, *the award-winning travel magazine.*

---

# THE HOTEL MANAGER

## Eugénie Jason

I always knew I wanted to travel the world, and working in the hotel industry has allowed me to do just that. I grew up in France, but I worked in hotels across the globe in destinations such as Monaco, London, Bora Bora, Beverly Hills, Washington, Montreal, and more before I landed in Halifax, where I am the general manager of the city's newest hotel, Muir. Muir is a luxurious 109-room hotel right on the gorgeous Nova Scotian waterfront, and since opening our doors in

December 2021, we've prided ourselves on giving our guests the best possible experience. That's one of the things I love about hotels: They are a theatre for people to make memories for a lifetime.

Of course, we also have guests who are travelling on business, and their stay is more transactional. In and out. They use the hotel to sleep, and they order the same burger wherever they are in the world. More and more, though, we see business travellers who also want to discover the city they are in. They might say, "This is my first time in Halifax. Where would you recommend I go for dinner? Where do the locals go?" They want to see their surroundings, dip their toes in the harbour, and enjoy some good food on a terrace instead of being alone. For these guests, we offer two-hour scenarios that they can enjoy between meetings.

With vacationers, we have a better opportunity to connect because they are here for a longer period and are usually more relaxed. They want to interact with us more because we are part of the local experience. They want to hear what we have to say about where we live, and about the best place for lobster. They're curious.

It's easy to say our goal is to make every guest happy, but that means we have to be on the ball all the time. I always tell the team at the hotel that just because a guest is quiet and friendly, and not screaming at us, it doesn't mean everything is okay. For example, if a family on vacation loses their luggage, that's a hassle, no matter how well they're handling it. And while technically, it's not our problem, we step in. We follow up with the airline on their behalf so they don't have to waste more time. We make sure that they get the personal amenities they need. We offer laundry service. We tell them about a little store nearby, where they can quickly pick up other necessities.

The hands-on customer service we offer at Muir is what makes our hotel luxurious—beyond the ocean view, bespoke furnishings, fitness centre, and other trappings. We want to show every guest that we value them. If they ask for something, as long as it's ethical and legal, we try to make it happen. When people ask for something that simply does not exist in Nova Scotia, it's an exciting challenge for us. We call other cities and see what we can do. If a guest wants a helicopter ride to a golf course, we'll try to negotiate that. Those are the details that make a luxury hotel truly one of a kind.

Managing a luxury hotel like Muir, I have to think quickly on my feet because I never know what's going to happen next. Like when I got a call about a "guest incident" on one of our floors. I raced up to the floor and saw three of my employees chasing around after a cat. It seems a guest went out and left their cat behind in the room, and when housekeeping opened the door, the cat escaped. It was like a scene from a movie. That doesn't happen every day, but I literally have time blocked in my schedule every day for a potential emergency. It may not be critical, but something always comes up. I never get bored because there's not a day like the day before.

The people component of the job is paramount. There are the guests, of course, to whom I must deliver a stellar experience that supports the rates we charge. But there are also my colleagues.

It takes a special kind of person to work in the hotel industry because of the hours. Often, we work weekends and holidays. So before we opened Muir, we looked for people who take a personal interest in hospitality, who do the job for more than a paycheque. In a luxury hotel where we prioritize the guest experience, we need all our employees to buy in to providing that level of service.

Of the staff at the hotel—housekeeping, front desk, plumbing, and more—I interviewed all but five. The interview process is crucial to

*Standing in our reception in November 2019, just weeks before our official opening. Behind me is one of our art pieces—a modern, traditionally inspired tapestry by Allison Pinsent Baker that captures the Nova Scotia landscape.*

finding talent because if we bring the wrong people to the team, it can have very negative impacts. I'm a strong believer that attitude is more important than the skills you may have. Skills, I can teach. Attitude, I cannot. If someone does not have the can-do gene in them, if they are not genuine and welcoming, I cannot teach that.

What I discovered is that even though Halifax didn't have many people trained to the level of service that we were trying to provide, many of our candidates had the right attitude—call it East Coast hospitality. So we brought them on, which meant we started from scratch in many areas and had to train, train, and train again. Now we have an exemplary team that offers a level of service on par with luxury hotels in any major city.

Everybody has a role to play. For example, when housekeeping goes to a guest's room, they pair the shoes, they fold everything they see very neatly, and they put a little card on the bed with a playlist the guest might enjoy listening to that night. We push the details. When a guest orders food for in-room dining, we don't just drop it off at the door. We create a true dining experience. We pull the chairs, pour the beverage, and pay attention to the view where the table is set up.

As the general manager, I have my hands in everything because I have to be sure we're running a successful and sustainable business model. Generating revenue means understanding the operation. It's important that I'm able to go from one topic to another very quickly. One moment, I could be dealing with finances, the next I might be dealing with a situation where an employee was treated rudely by a guest.

I teach my staff that they should be caring. My attitude is that we are all here to welcome and assist every guest. When a guest is a bit rude or abrupt, I advise my staff to try to not take the situation personally. We don't know what guests are going through. Maybe they had a meeting that didn't go well. Maybe they have a terrible boss. Maybe they just came back from visiting someone in the hospital who's not doing well. Still, it doesn't make their behaviour acceptable, so when these situations arise, I do confront the guest. It's not fun, but it's my job to protect the team when a guest doesn't act with the kindness and manners that are expected. And these conversations always end with an apology from the guest.

Each day, I get to the hotel at about eight a.m. I walk around a bit, peek into the sales office and say hi, and ask about anything juicy that's cooking. I'll make similar stops at the operations office, the gym (I check if the fruit is fresh), and the lobby (do any spots need paint touch-ups?). Then at nine a.m., we have a major staff meeting where we go over what's happening that day in the hotel and which guests are coming in. We also talk about the challenges from the day before. Mistakes can happen, but the important thing is to learn from them. I always say, "Let's peel the onion to get at the root of the problem." For example, a guest arrived before our check-in time of three p.m. If she arrived at eight a.m., it just may not be possible to find a room that's ready, but if she came at two p.m., and if we called her a few days before to check on her arrival time, and the room still was not ready, that's not good. Together, we brainstorm the steps we can take to make sure that every arrival is as smooth as butter. Our goal is a seamless arrival where we give the guest their keys, take them to their room, show them the beautiful features, and then that's it.

My job is demanding. There's no real downtime because the hotel is always open. I always have my phone with me, and it rings quite a bit. My weekends may end at five p.m. on Sunday because I have an event somewhere to promote the hotel. And my family has to be understanding of that. The hotel is like an extra chair at my dining room table. But I feel lucky to do what I do. I'm a woman in what is still a very male-dominated industry, and I'm showing others that it is possible to have a career and a family. I could have become a lawyer as my father hoped, but working in the hospitality industry is my dream come true. And I'm helping other people realize their dreams by providing the space and opportunity to make memories with the people they care about most.

## Postscript

*Eugénie Jason left the Muir hotel in July 2023 to be closer to her family in France. She is now the general manager of Les Bateaux Belmond, a company that offers luxury cruises on French rivers.*

# Acknowledgments

I first met Mark Bulgutch at the CBC in the 1980s, and we've had a wonderful partnership ever since. He was my writer, my lineup editor, my producer, and my executive producer for years of newscasts and news specials. His was a voice I trusted implicitly when he whispered breaking information in my ear during a live broadcast. And all these years later, I still trust him and depend on him, these days as a coauthor. This is our second book together, and if he can put up with me, I hope there will be more!

Sarah St. Pierre has been my editor at Simon & Schuster for three books now. How she's put up with me for even one is beyond me. But I know this: Without her, these books would never make it to print. She's a treasure. And Simon & Schuster publisher Kevin Hanson is the one who gambled his firm's reputation on me and I'm extremely grateful he gave me that chance. And my friend and producer Lara Chatterjee once again helped track down people and pictures, which were key to telling some of these stories.

My wife Cynthia is the last person I read these chapters to before pushing "send," and she always finds something to make them better.

But finally, the people who make this book are the people in it.

Their willingness and openness to tell their stories helped us find the path to how Canada works.

*Peter Mansbridge*
*Stratford, Ontario*

---

Millions of Canadians know Peter Mansbridge. Tens of Canadians know me. I've had a fine career working in his shadow. We've collaborated for forty years, through thousands of broadcasts and now two books. I picked a good shadow.

Simon & Schuster picked a good editor in Sarah St. Pierre. I like how she cut to the heart of everything we wrote and put these chapters into their final shape for you.

In writing my part of this book, I always had my father in my head. He had almost no formal education and worked his entire life as a manual labourer at a sugar refinery. I've always known that honest hard work was important to Canada.

I've also known for a very long time that family makes everything possible. With Rhonda, Melissa, Jessica, and Reid, my life has been enriched beyond reasonable expectation. If Peter provided shadow, they provided sunshine.

*Mark Bulgutch*
*Toronto, Ontario*

# Photo Credits

All photos are courtesy of the subjects, unless otherwise specified.

*Cover*
Wayne Moonias, left.
Christy Climenhaga, top-left.
Rechev Browne, top-center.
Eugénie Jason, top-right.
David Mitchell, bottom-right. Credit: Jan Michael Jurek
Amber Doiron, bottom-center. Credit: Nav Canada

*Interior*
Rob Wilson team picture. Credit: The Peterborough Petes
Rob Wilson NHL draft. Credit: The Peterborough Petes
Christy Climenhaga and Robert Grandjambe. Credit: Caitlin Hanson
Margaret Gallagher. Credit: Natasha MacKay
Patrick O'Brien. Credit: Parole Board of Canada
Danielle Cormier. Credit: The Canadian Space Agency
David Mitchell. Credit: Jan Michael Jurek
Valerie Blackmore. Credit: Wyndham Forensic Group

Lesley Thompson. Credit: Elise Cayouette

David Wiens. Credit: Ian Krahn

Deep Saini. Credit: Nick Pearce, Dalhousie University

Andrea Hounsell. Credit: Nate & Nichole Photography

Mike Nadajewski. Credit: Bruce Monk

Jennifer Ward. Credit: Dr. Julie Choi

# About the Authors

**Peter Mansbridge** is one of Canada's most respected journalists. He is the former chief correspondent for CBC News; anchor of *The National*, CBC's flagship nightly newscast, where he worked for thirty years reporting on national and international news stories; and host of *Mansbridge One on One*. He has received more than a dozen national awards for broadcast excellence, including a lifetime achievement award from the Academy of Canadian Cinema & Television. He is a distinguished fellow of the Munk School of Global Affairs & Public Policy at the University of Toronto and the former two-term chancellor of Mount Allison University. In 2008, he was made an officer of the Order of Canada—the country's highest civilian honour—and in 2012 he was awarded the Queen Elizabeth II Diamond Jubilee Medal. He is the author of the instant #1 national bestsellers *Off the Record* and *Extraordinary Canadians*, as well as the national bestseller *Peter Mansbridge*

*One on One: Favourite Conversations and the Stories Behind Them.* He lives in Stratford, Ontario. Follow him on X @PeterMansbridge, visit him at ThePeterMansbridge.com, or listen to his daily podcast, *The Bridge*, with Sirius XM Canada.

PHOTOGRAPH © JESSICA BULGUTCH

**Mark Bulgutch** is a journalist, educator, speaker, and the author of the instant #1 national bestseller *Extraordinary Canadians* and three other books. He worked for CBC for forty years, eleven as the senior editor of *The National* and another ten as senior executive producer of all live news specials. He taught at Toronto Metropolitan University for thirty-five years. A regular contributor of opinion columns to the *Toronto Star*, he has won fourteen Gemini Awards, four RTDNA Awards, the Canadian Journalism Foundation Award of Excellence, and the Canadian Association of Broadcasters Gold Ribbon Award. He lives in Toronto. Follow him on X @MarkBulgutch.